A-Z CHELM

Key to Map Pages	2-3
Map Pages	4-26
Large Scale Town Centre	27
Index t… Village… and se…	

REFERENCE

A Road	A12
B Road	B1137
Dual Carriageway	
One-way Street Traffic flow on A Roads is also indicated by a heavy line on the driver's left.	
Road Under Construction Opening dates are correct at the time of publication.	
Proposed Road	
Junction Name	SANDON INTERCHANGE
Restricted Access	
Pedestrianized Road	
Footpath	
Track	
Residential Walkway	
Railway	Level Crossing, Station, Tunnel
Built-up Area	QUEEN ST.
Local Authority Boundary	
Post Town Boundary	
Postcode Boundary (within Post Town)	
Map Continuation	14, Large Scale Town Centre 27
Car Park (selected)	P
Church or Chapel	†
Cycleway (selected)	
Fire Station	■
Hospital	H
House Numbers (A & B Roads only)	189 38
Information Centre	i
National Grid Reference	⁵70
Park and Ride	Sandon P+R
Police Station	▲
Post Office	★
Safety Camera with Speed Limit Fixed cameras and long term road works cameras. Symbols do not indicate camera direction.	30
Toilet: without facilities for the Disabled	
with facilities for the Disabled	
Disabled use only	
Educational Establishment	
Hospital or Healthcare Building	
Industrial Building	
Leisure or Recreational Facility	
Place of Interest	
Public Building	
Shopping Centre or Market	
Other Selected Buildings	

SCALE

Map Pages 4-26 1:19000

0 ¼ ½ Mile

0 250 500 750 Metres

3.33 inches (8.47cm) to 1 mile 5.26cm to 1 kilometre

Map Page 27 1:9500

0 ⅛ ¼ Mile

0 100 200 300 Metres

6.67 inches (16.94cm) to 1 mile 10.53cm to 1 kilometre

EDITION 5 2016

Telephone: 01732 781000 (Enquiries & Trade Sales)
01732 783422 (Retail Sales)

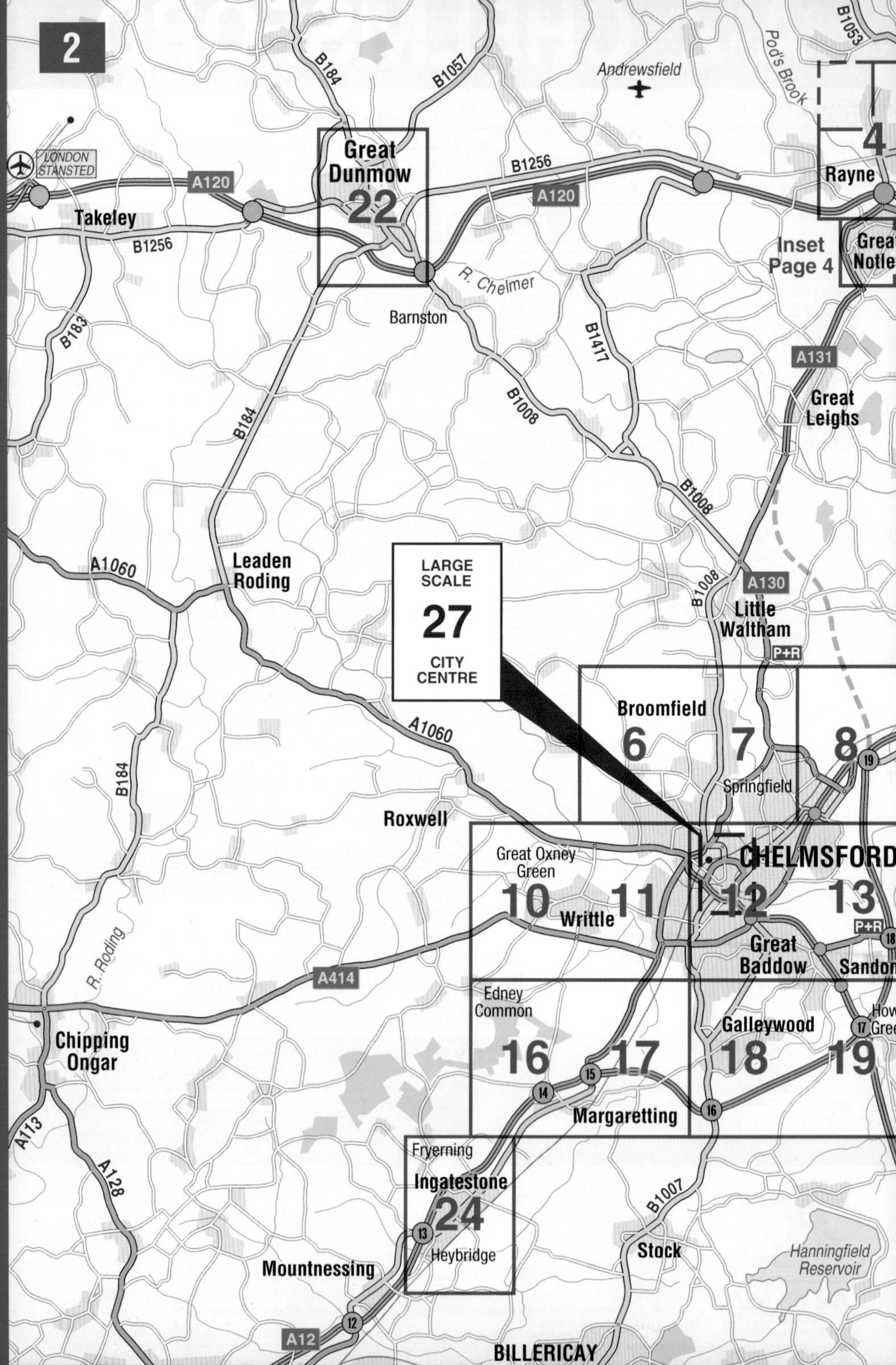

LONDON STANSTED
Takeley
A120
B1256
B184
B1057
Great Dunmow
22
Andrewsfield
Pod's Brook
B1053
4
Rayne
A120
Inset Page 4
Great Notley
R. Chelmer
Barnston
B183
B1417
B1008
A131
Great Leighs
B184
B1008
A1060
Leaden Roding
LARGE SCALE
27
CITY CENTRE
B1008
A130
Little Waltham
P+R
Broomfield
6
7
8
Springfield
A1060
B184
Roxwell
Great Oxney Green
CHELMSFORD
10
11
12
13
Writtle
P+R
R. Roding
A414
Great Baddow
Sandon
Edney Common
Chipping Ongar
Galleywood
16
17
18
19
Margaretting
A113
Fryerning
A128
Ingatestone
24
B1007
Heybridge
Stock
Hanningfield Reservoir
Mountnessing
A12
BILLERICAY

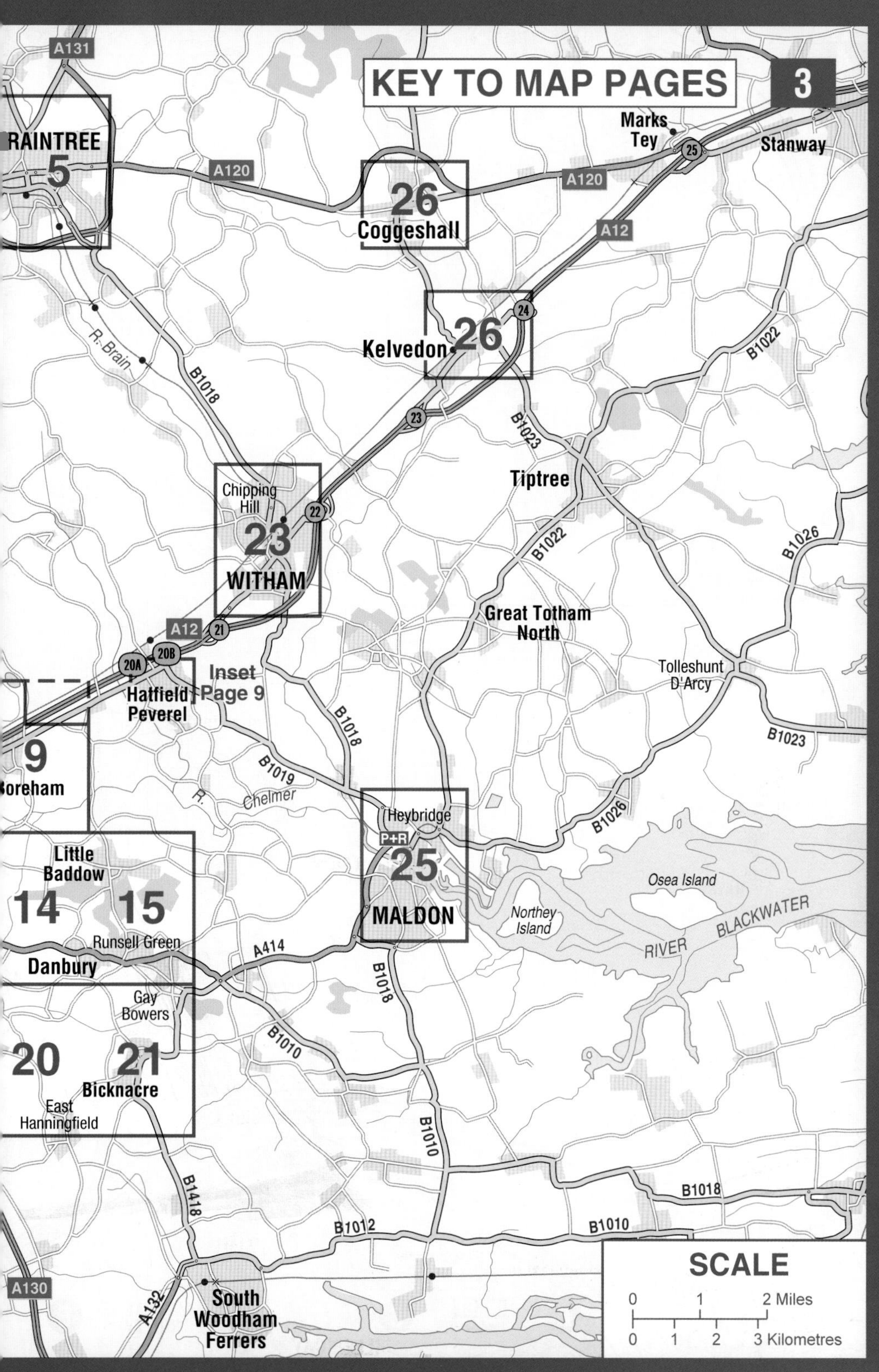

RAINTREE
5
A131
A120
26
Coggeshall
Marks Tey
25
Stanway
A12
24
26
Kelvedon
R. Brain
B1018
B1022
23
B1023
Tiptree
Chipping Hill
22
23
WITHAM
B1026
Great Totham North
A12
21
20A
20B
Hatfield Peverel
Inset Page 9
Tolleshunt D'Arcy
B1018
B1023
9
Boreham
B1019
R. Chelmer
Heybridge
P+R
25
B1026
Little Baddow
14
15
Runsell Green
MALDON
Osea Island
Northey Island
RIVER BLACKWATER
A414
Danbury
B1018
Gay Bowers
B1010
20
21
Bicknacre
East Hanningfield
B1010
B1418
B1018
B1012
B1010
A130
A132
South Woodham Ferrers
SCALE
0 1 2 Miles
0 1 2 3 Kilometres

4
INSET
Great Notley Country Park
The Discovery Centre
GREAT NOTLEY
Braintree
CM77
White Court Prim. Sch.
Superstore
Nursery
Play. Field
Longmead
Depot
Friaries
Peacehaven
Cards
The Barn
A131
Reservoir
Matthew's Farm
Park Farm
Recycling Centre
Edith Borthwick School
Braintree Enterprise Cen.
Colchester Institute
Tabor Academy
Leisure Centre
Running Track
Playing Field
Reservoir (covered)
John Bunyan Jun. & Inf. Schs.
St. Michael's Hospital
Braintree Comm. Hosp.
Springwood Industrial Estate
Rayne Lodge
Rayne Lodge Fishery
Clap Bridge
Pump House
The Pines
Rayne Hall
Rayne Hall Ind. Est.
War Memorial
Rayne Hall Farm
RAYNE
Sports Ground
Gilda Terrace
Broomhills Ind. Est.
Prim. Sch.
Cemetery
Millhouse
Marshalls Park
Bridge Farm
Piggery
Notley Cross
Greensleeves
Naylinghurst
Braintree Green
Springett
Payling Cottages
Wenas Farm
Tyeponds
Fairy Hall
Cottage Acre
Stanford Farm
Two Hoots
Little Bishops
Queenborough Meadow
Lakes Farm
Little Common
Spinners
Skyline 120
Hill House Farm
Hill House Cottage
A120
B1256
Rayne Road
Pods Brook Rd.
Queenborough La.
London Road
Coldnailhurst Avenue
Panfield La.
Acorn Avenue
Clare Road
Shalford Rd.
Gore Rd.
Queenborough La.
A B C D E
1 2 3 4 5 6 7

5
76
77
78
F
G
H
J
K
1
2
3
4
5
6
7
25
24
23
22
Thistley Green
THISTLEY GREEN RD.
CYPRESS GARDENS
A131
B1053
BROAD ROAD
CONVENT HILL
Highfield Stile Farm
HIGHFIELD STILE RD.
Works
Sewage Works
Boleyn's Farm
Colchester Institute
Bradford Bri.
BRADFORD ST.
CONVENT LANE
THE CLOISTERS
River Blackwater
Darby's Hole
Bocking Hole
Bocking
CM7
CHURCH LANE
POLLY'S HILL
CHURCH ST.
BOLEYNS AV.
EAGLE LA.
MAYSENT AV.
FAGGOT YARD
TENTER CL.
BEECH AV.
ANDREW CL.
AVENUE
GRIMSHAW
ST. JAMES CT.
SIX BELLS CT.
KINGFISHER GA.
PHILLIPS CHASE
WOOLPACK
FRIARS LA.
BRADFORD ST.
RIVER
BLACKWATER WY.
VALLEY ROAD
HOLLY WY.
BROOK
COURTAULD
JULIEN COURT ROAD
Public Gardens
Tennis Courts
Howard Hall
BOCKING END
ST. PETER'S RD.
Offs.
Playing Field
Recreation Ground
Tennis Courts
Pav.
BRAINTREE
Playing Fields
B1256
COGGESHALL ROAD
Great Bradfords Jun. & Inf. Schs.
MARLBOROUGH
CONNAUGHT
GARDENS
YORK
KENT
CORNWALL GDNS.
GLOUCESTER
EDINBURGH GDNS.
MOUNTBATTEN
TRAFALGAR
WELLINGTON CL.
BOSCAWEN GDS.
BALMORAL CT.
FALKLAND CT.
WARWICK
WESTMINSTER
RUTLAND
NORFOLK
PORTLAND
COLLINGWOOD
ALBEMARLE GDNS.
GILBERT WY.
NORRIS CL.
CAVENDISH GS.
VERNON
BRIDPORT WAY
HEREFORD
NORTHAMPTON
BOURCHIER
STAFFORD
DEERLEAP WY.
SOVEREIGN
GUNEA
FARTHING
Sch.
KEYES WY.
DRAKE GS.
HAWKINS WY.
NELSON
FROBISHER
BEATTY
KINGSMEAD CARAVAN PARK
HARWELL
WILLINGALE RD
ROCHESTER
DUNOON
BROADOAKS
TIDESWELL
Moat
A120
COGGESHALL ROAD
MARKS ROUNDABOUT
Superstore
TWELVE ACRES
BOTANY DR.
GULLS CROFT
CRABS CROFT
LIE FIELD CL.
KITCHEN FIELD
MARTENS
MEADOW
PEARL DR.
BRAIDING CRES.
PLAITERS WAY
LAMMAS
BLACK BREAD CL.
DUNSTABLE DR.
Ley Wood
King George's Field
Comm. Cen.
Templeborder Wood
HOWARD CL.
CUNNINGTON RD.
WHEATLEY AV.
AVENUE
HAY LANE
THORPE M.
BARTRAM
MARKS
WARREN
WARREN RD.
RUSTIC CL.
BADGER GRO.
WOODLANDS
BEAUMONT PL.
CRESSING ROAD
ST. MARY'S RD.
TROTTERS FIELD
Ind. Estate
BISHOPS AV.
CLOCKHOUSE WY.
STUARTS WY.
CHAPEL HILL
HARTLEY HO.
Club
Pav.
Braintree Town FC (Avanti Stadium)
Bowl Grn.
THE CHASEWAY
Ten. Cts.
Play. Field
Alec Hunter Academy
STUBBS LA.
HAYTOR CL.
HUNTER DR.
SALCOMBE RD.
CHERITON RD.
KNIGHTS RD.
Playing Field
Works
THAMES RD.
CHELMER
CROUCH CT.
COLNE
THE SPINNEY
FRATING CT.
MUNDON RD.
BRADWELL CT.
GOLDHANGER CT.
LEYWOOD CL.
Prim. Sch.
BRICK KILN WY.
TEMPLAR RD.
CRUSADER
TAPESTRY WK.
GREEN
THE LEY
BECKERS
PLAINS FIELD
MIDDLE KING
KING CRESS
PUNDERS FLD.
SLOUGH HO. CL.
LEA CL.
GALLEY ROUNDABOUT
Cressing Lodge
LONG GREEN
GALLEYS CORNER
Depots
Garden Centre
Sub.
B1018 RD.
BRAINTREE
Hoppit House
CM77
Brain
ALBERT RD.
MALTINGS LA.
KEEBLE WY.
RAILWAY ST.
MANOR ST.
THE WOODFIELD
Superstore
Mus.
Braintree Bus Sta.
Lib.
VICTORIA
ALEXANDRA
TRINOVANTIAN WAY
GROSVENOR
SOUTH STREET
B1256
MAZERS CT.
DAMASK M.
STATION APPROACH
ROSE HILL
ROSE GDS.
HOLDEN
Gasholder Station
ENTERPRISE
LAKES RD.
MANOR ST.
BENFIELD WY.
LAKES INDUSTRIAL PARK
ANGLIA WY.
Works
Braintree
THE WATERINGS
ST. JOHN'S AV.
SHOOTERS WY.
SPLASH CT.
AIRMONT CL.
Hoppit Bridge
RIFLE HILL
APPLETREE WLK.
PEARTREE CL.
STRAWBERRY CL.
THE RIDGEWAY
PERRY FIELDS
HILLSIDE
STEPHENSON RD.
ORCHARD DRIVE
BRUNEL RD.
WORCESTER
Playing Field
HOPPIT MEAD
JENNER CL.
LODGE RD.
FARADAY CL.
NEWTON CL.
EDISON
LISTER
BUCKWOODS RD.
BEADON
NINEACRES
BRAMLEY
RUSSET CL.
CHALLIS LANE
DAVIES CT.
MILL HILL
ANGLE SIDE
MEGS
SEDGEFIELD WY.
DUGGERS LA.
LONG ACRES
THE LINDENS
Weirs
BULRUSH CL.
CENTURY DR.
MILLENNIUM WAY
FREEPORT OFFICE VILLAGE
FREEPORT BRAINTREE
Braintree Freeport
CHARTER WY.
Namco Funscape
BRAINTREE RETAIL PARK
Braintree Swimming Centre
Cineworld
B1018
RUSHMOOR DRIVE
RYE GRASS WY.
WOODRUSH CL.
SKITTS HILL IND. EST.
DRIBERG WY.
HARRISON DR.
BARLEY CT.
REED MDWS.
PUTTER CT.
BAMBOO CRES.
Factory
Works
River
Sewage Works
COWPAR MEWS
PENN M.
LEONARD
INGRAM M.
HITCHAM M.
PARK DRIVE
FORSYTH
CONNDYLE
AUSTEN
BRONTE
GREENE WY.
A120
KEATS AV.
BETJEMAN
HIGH ELMS
MASEFIELD RD.
CHAUCER
BYRON CL.
BROWNING RD.
KIPLING
DICKENS CL.
THACKERAY CL.
SCOTT
GOLDINGHAM
HARDY CL.
LONGLEAF DR.
BUCHAN CL.
BENNETT
LOWE
SWIFT
JOHNSON
SHAKESPEARE
BLACK NOTLEY LODGE
ROAD
John Ray Jun. & Inf. Schs.
Play. Fld.
Playing Field

6
A
B
C
D
E
68
69
11
210
09
08
1
2
3
4
5
6
7
CHIGNALL ROAD
BREEDS ROAD
Maple View
Ford
Woodhall Farm
WOODHALL HILL
Gray's Farm
Greenfields
Woodside
CHIGNAL ROAD
Bushy Wood
Partridge Green Cottages
The Christopher Unit
THE LINDEN C
Partridge Green
Stacey's Farm
Scravels
Parsona Green
Nurseries
MASHBURY ROAD
Brittons Hall Farm
Brittons
Broomwood Lodge
Broom Wood
Beaumont Otes
Chobbing's Farm
HOLLOW ROAD
The Blue House
Priors
Scot's Green
Claypits Cottages
CM1
Daffy Wood
Brickbarns Cottages
Brickbarns Farm
COPPERFIELD ROAD
Lib. Sch.
Superstore
Comm. Cen.
Chelmsford Sport & Athletic Cen.
Chelmsford City FC (Melbourne Stadium)
College Wood
Melbourne Park
Playing Field
Pav.
Play. Fld.
Parkwood Acad.
MELBOURNE AVENUE
PARTRIDGE AVENUE
School
Playgrd.
Hall
Tennis Courts
11
River Can

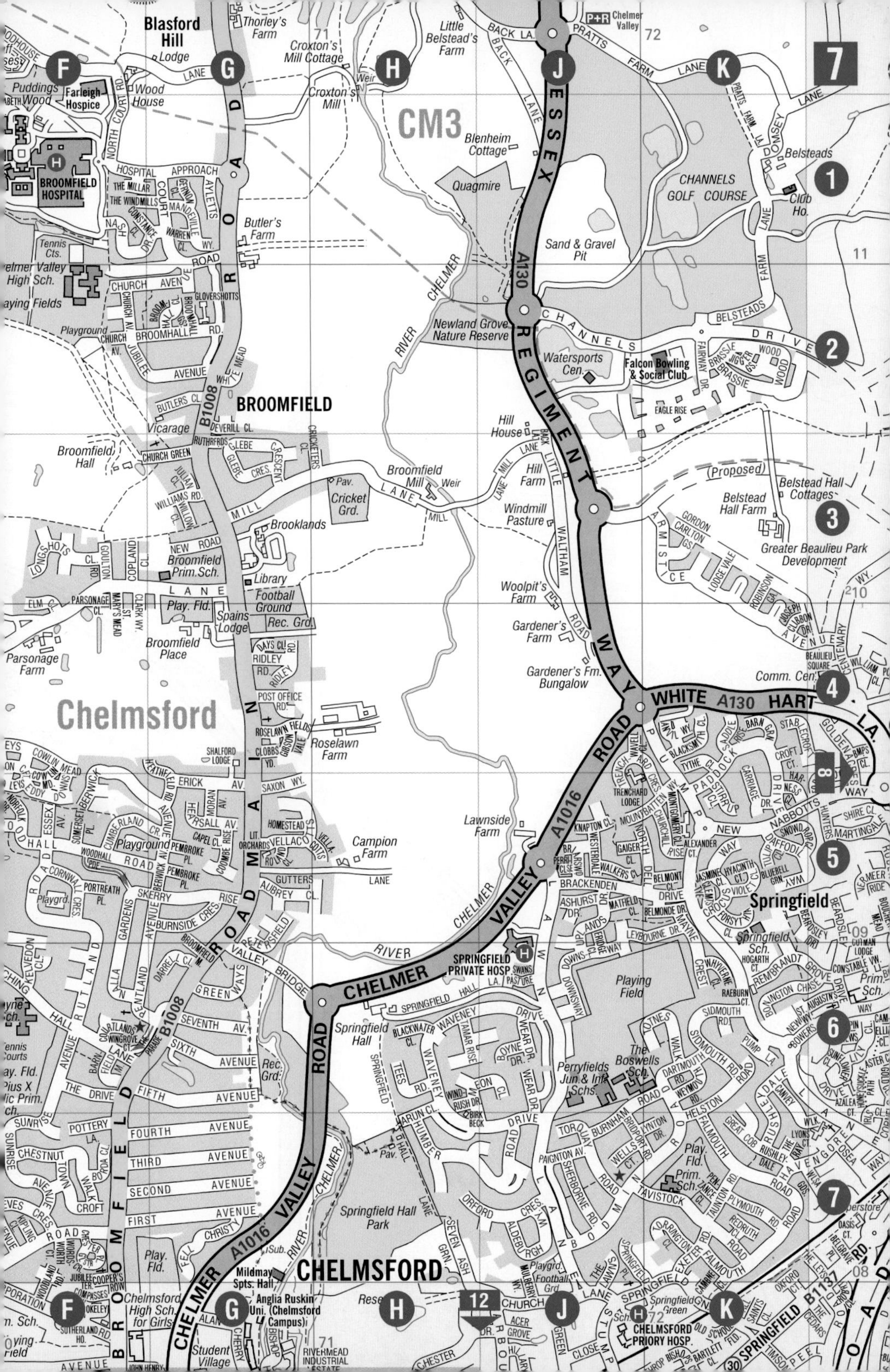
7
CM3
Blasford Hill
Lodge
Thorley's Farm
Croxton's Mill Cottage
Little Belstead's Farm
P+R Chelmer Valley
BACK LA.
PRATTS FARM LANE
Puddings Wood
Farleigh Hospice
Wood House
Croxton's Mill
Weir
Blenheim Cottage
Belsteads
CHANNELS GOLF COURSE
Club Ho.
BROOMFIELD HOSPITAL
HOSPITAL APPROACH
Quagmire
Butler's Farm
Sand & Gravel Pit
ESSEX REGIMENT WAY
A130
Tennis Cts.
Chelmer Valley High Sch.
Playing Fields
RIVER CHELMER
Newland Grove Nature Reserve
CHANNELS DRIVE
BELSTEADS
Watersports Cen.
Falcon Bowling & Social Club
EAGLE RISE
Playground
BROOMFIELD
B1008
Vicarage
Broomfield Hall
CHURCH GREEN
Hill House
Hill Farm
(Proposed)
Belstead Hall Cottages
Belstead Hall Farm
Broomfield Mill
Cricket Grd.
Brooklands
Windmill Pasture
Greater Beaulieu Park Development
Broomfield Prim.Sch.
Library
Football Ground
Rec. Grd.
Play. Fld.
Spains Lodge
Woolpit's Farm
Gardener's Farm
Gardener's Fm. Bungalow
Parsonage Farm
Broomfield Place
Comm. Cen.
Chelmsford
WHITE HART LA.
Roselawn Farm
Lawnside Farm
Campion Farm
Playground
Playgrd.
Springfield
Springfield Sch.
SPRINGFIELD PRIVATE HOSP
CHELMER VALLEY ROAD
A1016
Playing Field
Springfield Hall
Perryfields Jun.& Inf. Schs.
The Boswells Sch.
Rec. Grd.
Springfield Hall Park
Play. Fld.
Prim. Sch.
Play. Fld.
Mildmay Spts. Hall
CHELMSFORD
Anglia Ruskin Uni. (Chelmsford Campus)
Chelmsford High Sch. for Girls
Student Village
RIVERMEAD INDUSTRIAL ESTATE
Springfield Green
CHELMSFORD PRIORY HOSP.
SPRINGFIELD
B1137
12
8
71
72
11
10
09
08

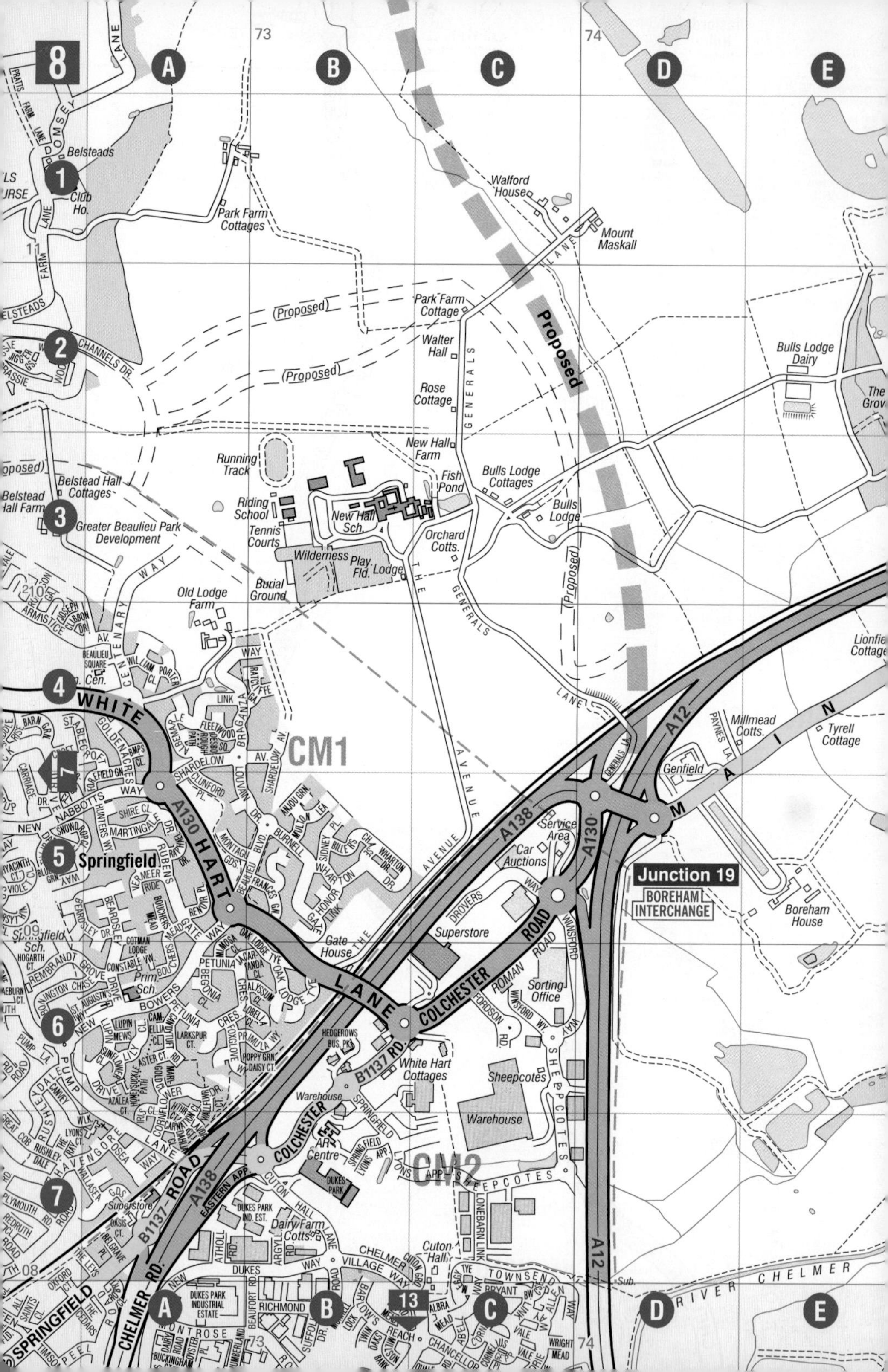

8
A
B
C
D
E
73
74
1
2
3
4
5
6
7
11
210
109
08
Belsteads
Club Ho.
Park Farm Cottages
Walford House
Mount Maskall
(Proposed)
Proposed
Park Farm Cottage
Walter Hall
Rose Cottage
New Hall Farm
GENERALS
Bulls Lodge Dairy
Bulls Lodge Cottages
Bulls Lodge
Fish Pond
Running Track
Belstead Hall Cottages
Belstead Hall Farm
Greater Beaulieu Park Development
Riding School
New Hall Sch.
Tennis Courts
Orchard Cotts.
Wilderness
Play Fld.
Lodge
Burial Ground
Old Lodge Farm
THE GENERALS
THE AVENUE
CHANNELS DR.
CENTENARY WAY
ARMISTICE AV.
BEAULIEU SQUARE
WILLIAM PORTER CL.
WHITE HART LANE
A130
A138
A12
CM1
CM2
Springfield
Springfield Sch.
Prim. Sch.
BEAULIEU BLVD.
BURNELL
WHARTON
GENERALS LA.
Genfield
Millmead Cotts.
Tyrell Cottage
Lionfield Cottage
PAYNES LA.
MAIN
Service Area
Car Auctions
DROVERS WAY
Superstore
Gate House
Junction 19
BOREHAM INTERCHANGE
Boreham House
COLCHESTER ROAD
ROMAN ROAD
WINSFORD
Sorting Office
FORDSON RD.
SHEEPCOTES
White Hart Cottages
HEDGEROWS BUS. PK.
B1137 RD.
Warehouse
Sheepcotes
Art Centre
DUKES PARK
SPRINGFIELD LYONS APP.
EASTERN APP.
CUTON HALL LANE
DUKES PARK IND. EST.
Dairy Farm Cotts.
Cuton Hall
CHELMER VILLAGE WAY
TOWNSEND
LONEBARN LINK
B1137 ROAD
CHELMER RD.
DUKES PARK INDUSTRIAL ESTATE
RICHMOND
BEAUFORT RD.
MONTROSE
13
RIVER CHELMER
Sub.
SPRINGFIELD
HAVENGORE
PUMP LA.
BOWERS
PETUNIA
Superstore
The Grove

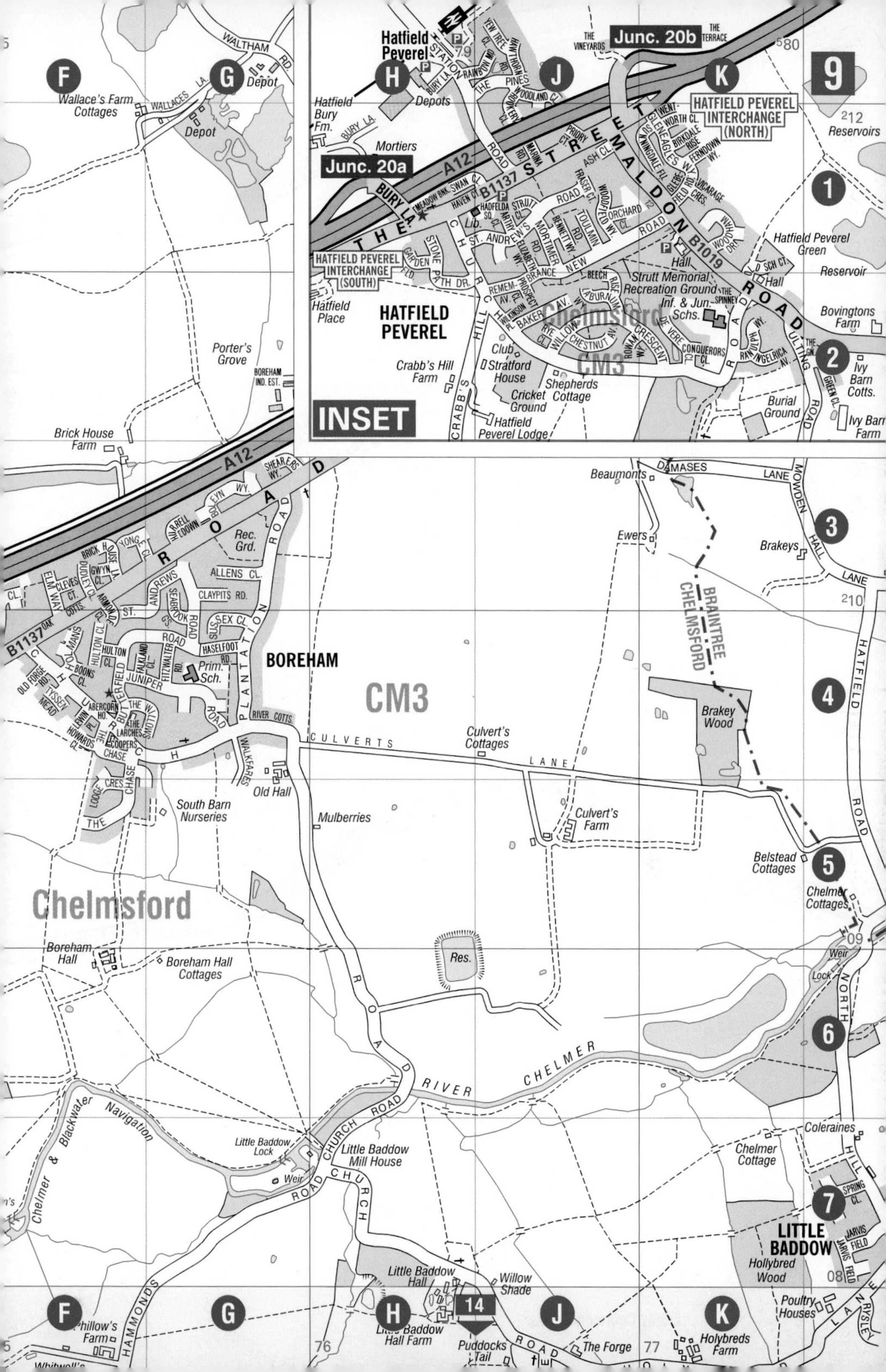
INSET
Hatfield Peverel
HATFIELD PEVEREL
Junc. 20a
Junc. 20b
HATFIELD PEVEREL INTERCHANGE (NORTH)
HATFIELD PEVEREL INTERCHANGE (SOUTH)
A12
B1137
B1019
THE STREET
MALDON ROAD
BURY LA.
STATION RD.
CHURCH HILL
CRABB'S HILL
NEW ROAD
ST. ANDREW'S ROAD
ULTING ROAD
Hatfield Bury Fm.
Mortiers
Depots
Hatfield Place
Crabb's Hill Farm
Stratford House
Cricket Ground
Shepherds Cottage
Hatfield Peverel Lodge
Strutt Memorial Recreation Ground
Inf. & Jun. Schs.
Hall
Lib.
Burial Ground
Ivy Barn Cotts.
Ivy Barn Farm
Bovingtons Farm
Hatfield Peverel Green
Reservoir
Reservoirs
The Vineyards
The Terrace
Wallace's Farm Cottages
WALLACES LA.
WALTHAM RD.
Depot
Porter's Grove
BOREHAM IND. EST.
Brick House Farm
BOREHAM
Rec. Grd.
Prim. Sch.
PLANTATION ROAD
CHURCH ROAD
RIVER COTTS.
Old Hall
South Barn Nurseries
Chelmsford
Boreham Hall
Boreham Hall Cottages
CM3
CULVERTS LANE
Culvert's Cottages
Culvert's Farm
Mulberries
Res.
DAMASES LANE
Beaumonts
Ewers
MOWDEN HALL LANE
Brakeys
BRAINTREE
CHELMSFORD
Brakey Wood
HATFIELD ROAD
Belstead Cottages
Chelmer Cottages
Weir
Lock
NORTH HILL
RIVER CHELMER
Chelmer & Blackwater Navigation
Little Baddow Lock
Little Baddow Mill House
CHURCH ROAD
HAMMONDS ROAD
Little Baddow Hall
Willow Shade
Little Baddow Hall Farm
Puddocks Tail
The Forge
Holybreds Farm
Coleraines
Chelmer Cottage
LITTLE BADDOW
Hollybred Wood
Poultry Houses
RYSLEY LANE
Phillow's Farm
14
F
G
H
J
K
1
2
3
4
5
6
7
76
77
580
212
210
209
208

10
VICARAGE
Galleons Hill
Thatcher's Farm
Broadacre
ROAD
Blackwall Bridge
Roxwell
ROXWELL
A1060
Reed's Spring
River Can
STREET
Thatchers Cottages
Hoestreet Cottages
Brook
Hoestreet
Moat
Little Thatchers Farm
LANE
HOE
Reservoir
The Hickerage
OLD
ROXWELL
Thieves' Corner
ROAD
Cattle Breeding Centre
The Orchards
Cader Idris
Whitesmiths
Stradella
Reeds Farm
Reeds Cottage
Orchard House
Hillcroft
GRAVELLY
WATERING
Writtle College (Sturgeons College)
Spinney House
Jubilee Farm
Newney Hall
Newney Green
Christophers
Moor Hall Cottages
Writtle College (Cow Watering Campus)
Sturgeons Cottages
COW
Reservoir
CM1
Moor Hall
Moat
VICTORIA
Clovers
Hassenbrook
Daws Farm
DAWS CL.
BLACKTHORN CL.
MAYFIELD
BACK ROAD
ROAD
Sand & Gravel Pit
FOSTERS CL.
EAST
TOWER RD.
Recreation Ground
LONGMEADS CL.
PURCELL COLE
Great Oxney Green
VIEW
MANSFIELDS
REDWOOD DR.
Comm. Cen.
HOME MEAD
SAWNEY BROOK
WELLFIELD
Bulimers Farm
Bush House
Depot
LONG
GREAT GODFREYS
CHEQUERS
OXNEY HO.
OXNEY MD.
ROLLESTONS
LITTLE STILE
RYLE
THE FURTHER MEADOW
BRAND
A414
Range Cottage
Grove House
Prospect Cottages
THE SHRUBBERIES
HIGHWOOD
ROAD
HIGHWOOD RD.
LODGE
Writtle Jun. & Inf. Schools
ONGAR
ROAD
Little Oxney Green
GREEN
New Rollestons Farm
Little Moor Hall
Ladygrove
Causeway Cottages
CHASE
Lady Grove
HIGHWOOD
CAUSEWAY
Halfway House
Roper's Farm
ROPER'S
Britleys
Lee Cottages
Warehouse
Montpelier's Farm
Moat
Sandy
Lee Wood
Lee Farm
Montpelier's Cottages
Phillips Farm
Bramwood Farm
Argents Nurseries
ROAD
THE
MARGARETTING
LANE
Bumpstead's Farm
Playing Field
Edney Common
16
HIGHWOOD
NATHAN'S LA.
NATHAN'S
Gable Cottages
Lodge
565
66
67
08
07
06
05
1
2
3
4
5
6
7
A
B
C
D
E

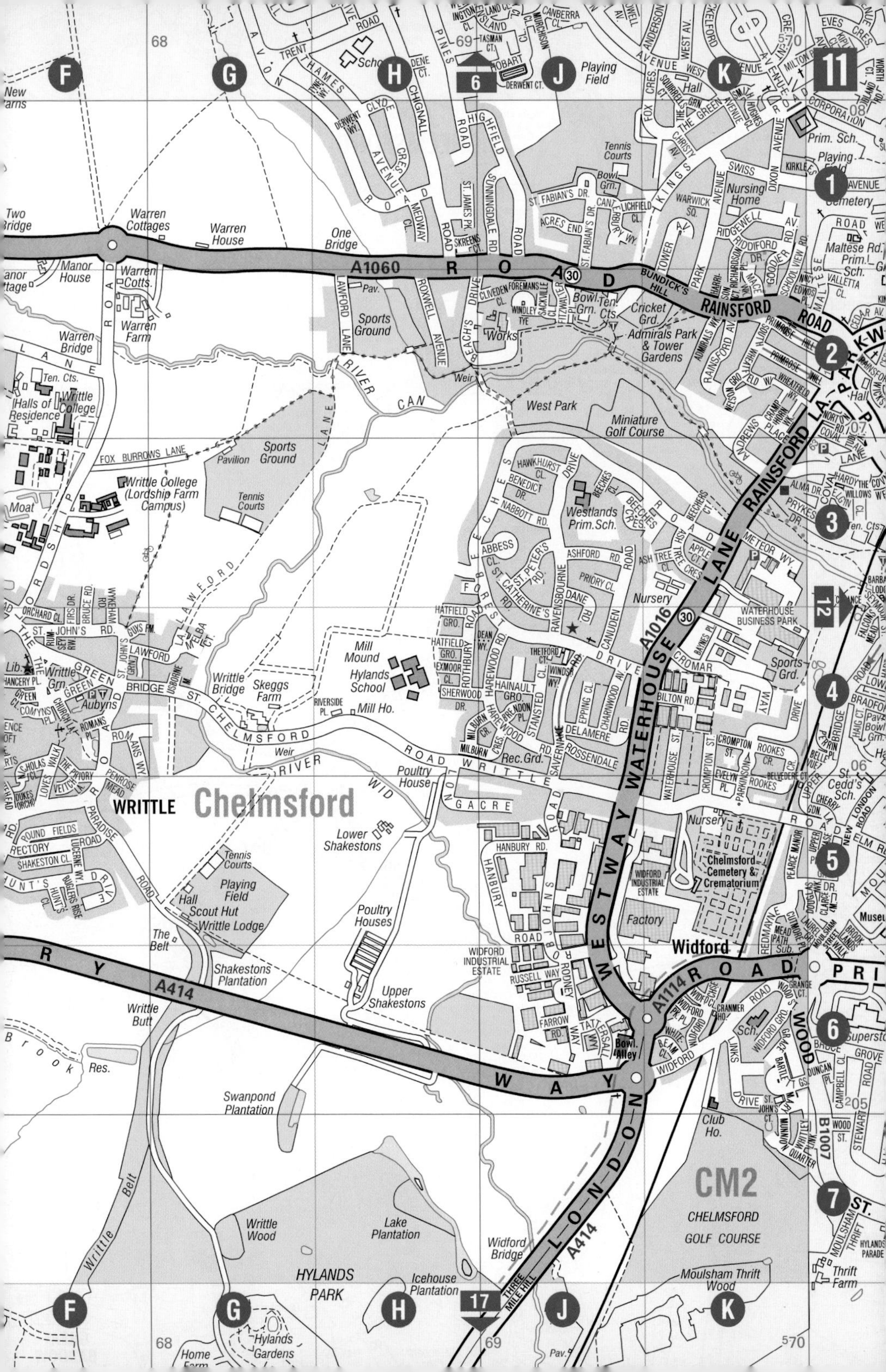

11
Chelmsford
WRITTLE
CM2
A1060 ROAD
RAINSFORD ROAD
A414
A1016
WESTWAY WATERHOUSE LANE
A1114 ROAD
LONDON
CHELMSFORD GOLF COURSE
HYLANDS PARK
West Park
Miniature Golf Course
Admirals Park & Tower Gardens
Writtle College
Writtle College (Lordship Farm Campus)
Hylands School
Westlands Prim.Sch.
Chelmsford Cemetery & Crematorium
Widford
WIDFORD INDUSTRIAL ESTATE
WATERHOUSE BUSINESS PARK
Warren Farm
Warren House
Warren Cottages
Manor House
Skeggs Farm
Lower Shakestons
Upper Shakestons
Poultry Houses
Swanpond Plantation
Writtle Wood
Lake Plantation
Icehouse Plantation
Moulsham Thrift Wood
Widford Bridge
Hylands Gardens
Thrift Farm
RIVER CAN
RIVER WID
6
12
17
68
69
570

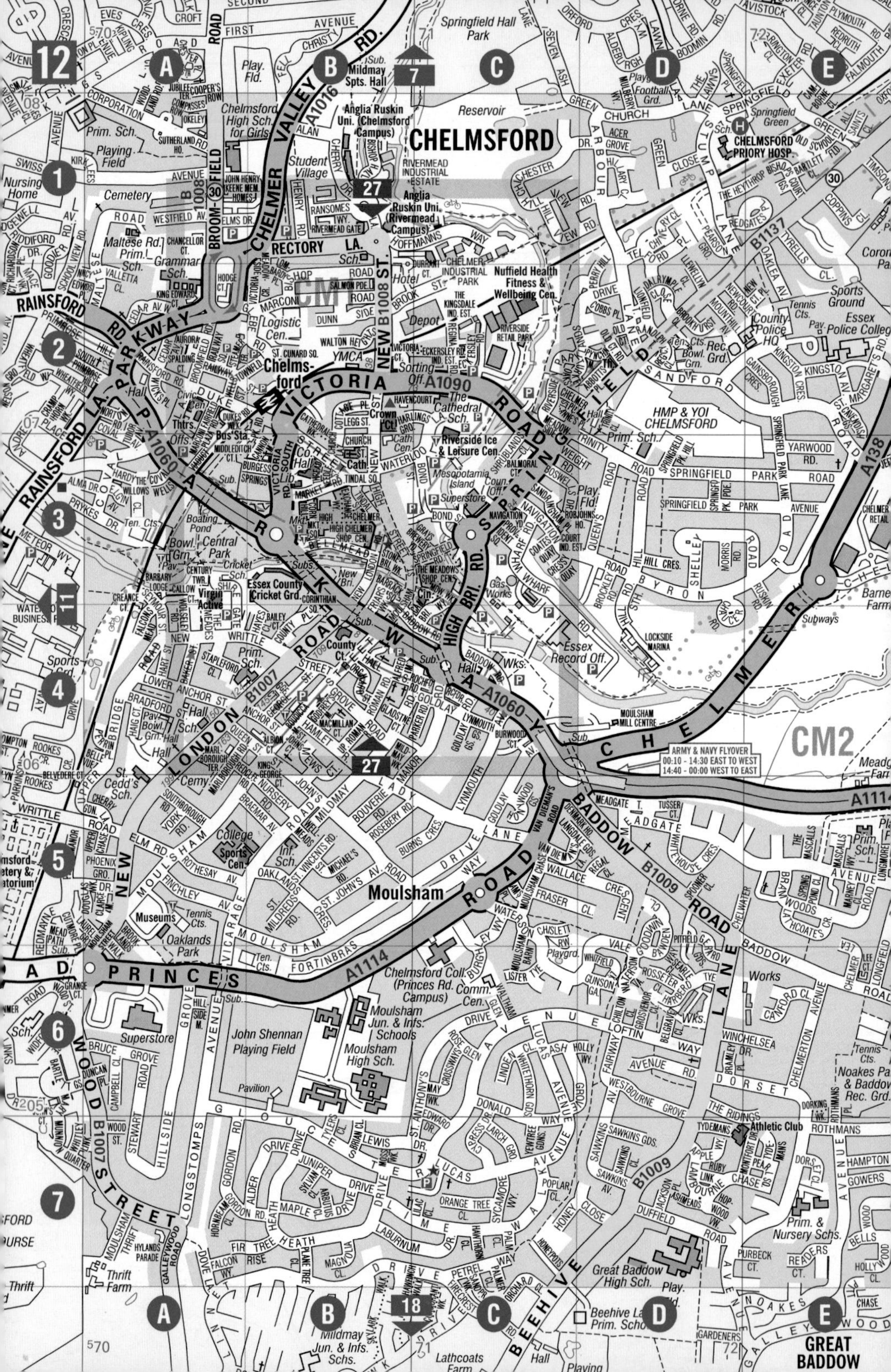

12
A
B
C
D
E
1
2
3
4
5
6
7
7
27
11
18
30
CHELMSFORD
CM1
CM2
Moulsham
GREAT BADDOW
Springfield Hall Park
Reservoir
Anglia Ruskin Uni. (Chelmsford Campus)
Student Village
RIVERMEAD INDUSTRIAL ESTATE
Anglia Ruskin Uni. (Rivermead Campus)
Mildmay Spts. Hall
Chelmsford High Sch. for Girls
Play. Fld.
Playing Field
Prim. Sch.
Nursing Home
Cemetery
Maltese Rd. Prim. Sch.
Grammar Sch.
JOHN HENRY KEENE MEM. HOMES
CHELMER INDUSTRIAL PARK
Nuffield Health Fitness & Wellbeing Cen.
THE KINGSDALE IND. EST.
RIVERSIDE RETAIL PARK
Depot
Logistic Cen.
YMCA
Sorting Off.
Chelmsford
Civic Cen.
Thtrs
Offs.
Bus Sta.
Crown Ct.
The Cathedral Sch.
Cath. Cen.
Cath.
Co. Hall
Lib.
Riverside Ice & Leisure Cen.
Mesopotamia Island
Superstore
Coun. Off.
HIGH CHELMER SHOP. CEN.
THE MEADOWS SHOP. CEN.
Cin.
New Bri.
Gas Works
Boating Pond
Central Park
Bowl. Grn.
Cricket Sch.
Virgin Active
Essex County Cricket Grd.
County Ct.
Essex Record Off.
Wks.
LOCKSIDE MARINA
MOULSHAM MILL CENTRE
HMP & YOI CHELMSFORD
Prim. Sch.
Play. Fld.
Rec. Grd.
County Police HQ
Essex Police College
Sports Ground
Tennis Cts.
CHELMSFORD PRIORY HOSP.
Springfield Green
Playg. Football Grd.
WATERHOUSE BUSINESS PARK
Sports Grd.
St. Cedd's Sch.
Cemy.
College Sports Cen.
Inf. Sch.
Museums
Oaklands Park
Chelmsford Coll. (Princes Rd. Campus)
Comm. Cen.
Moulsham Jun. & Infs. Schools
Moulsham High Sch.
John Shennan Playing Field
Pavilion
Superstore
Works
Noakes Pa & Baddow Rec. Grd.
Athletic Club
Prim. & Nursery Schs.
Great Baddow High Sch.
Beehive La Prim. Sch.
Mildmay Jun. & Infs. Schs.
Thrift Farm
Lathcoats Farm
Barnes Farm
Meadg Farm
Subways
ARMY & NAVY FLYOVER
00:10 - 14:30 EAST TO WEST
14:40 - 00:00 WEST TO EAST
VICTORIA ROAD
CHELMER VALLEY RD.
PARKWAY
PRINCES ROAD
BADDOW ROAD
NEW LONDON ROAD
HIGH BRI. RD.
SPRINGFIELD ROAD
RAINSFORD LA.
RAINSFORD RD.
MOULSHAM STREET
WOOD STREET
CHELMER
A1016
A1060
A1090
A1114
A138
B1007
B1008
B1009
B1137
570
571
572

13
8
14
19
F
G
H
J
K
1
2
3
4
5
6
7
08
07
06
205
74
575
73
Chelmer Village
Chelmsford
CM3
Sandon
SANDON
Lower Green
Junction 18
SANDON INTERCHANGE
A12
A1060
A414
A1114
MALDON ROAD
MALDON RD.
CHELMER WAY
VILLAGES WAY
SANDFORD ROAD
SANDFORD MILL ROAD
BROOK END ROAD
MILL LANE
HAMMONDS ROAD
GRACE'S WALK
WOODHILL ROAD
BRICK KILN ROAD
MOLRAMS LANE
CHURCH STREET
RIVER CHELMER
Chelmer & Blackwater Navigation
Dukes Park Industrial Estate
Dairy Farm Cotts.
Cuton Hall
Cuton Lock
Weir
Reservoir
Reservoirs
Chancellor Park Sports Area
Barnes Farm Jun. & Inf. Schs.
Superstore
Prim. Sch.
Brookend
Brook End Gardens
Sewage Works
Pease Hall
Prentice's Farm
Barnes Lock
Mill
Sandford Lock
Sandford Mill Bridge
Water Works
Mill Cottages
Manor Farm
Hammond's Cottages
Hammond's Farm
Rumbold's Farm
Rumbold's
Potash Cotts.
Grace's Cross
Brick Kiln Cottage
Playing Field
Playing Fields
The Sandon Sch.
Sandon Place
Sandon Centre
Hall Playing Field
The Rectory
Plumping Bridge
Sand & Gravel Pit
Sandon Lodge
Bridge Farm
Recreation Ground
Baddow Hall Jun. & Inf. Schs.
Tennis Court
Tennis Club
Depot
Pitt Place
Stonham's Lock
Phillow's Cotta
Sandon Brook
P+R

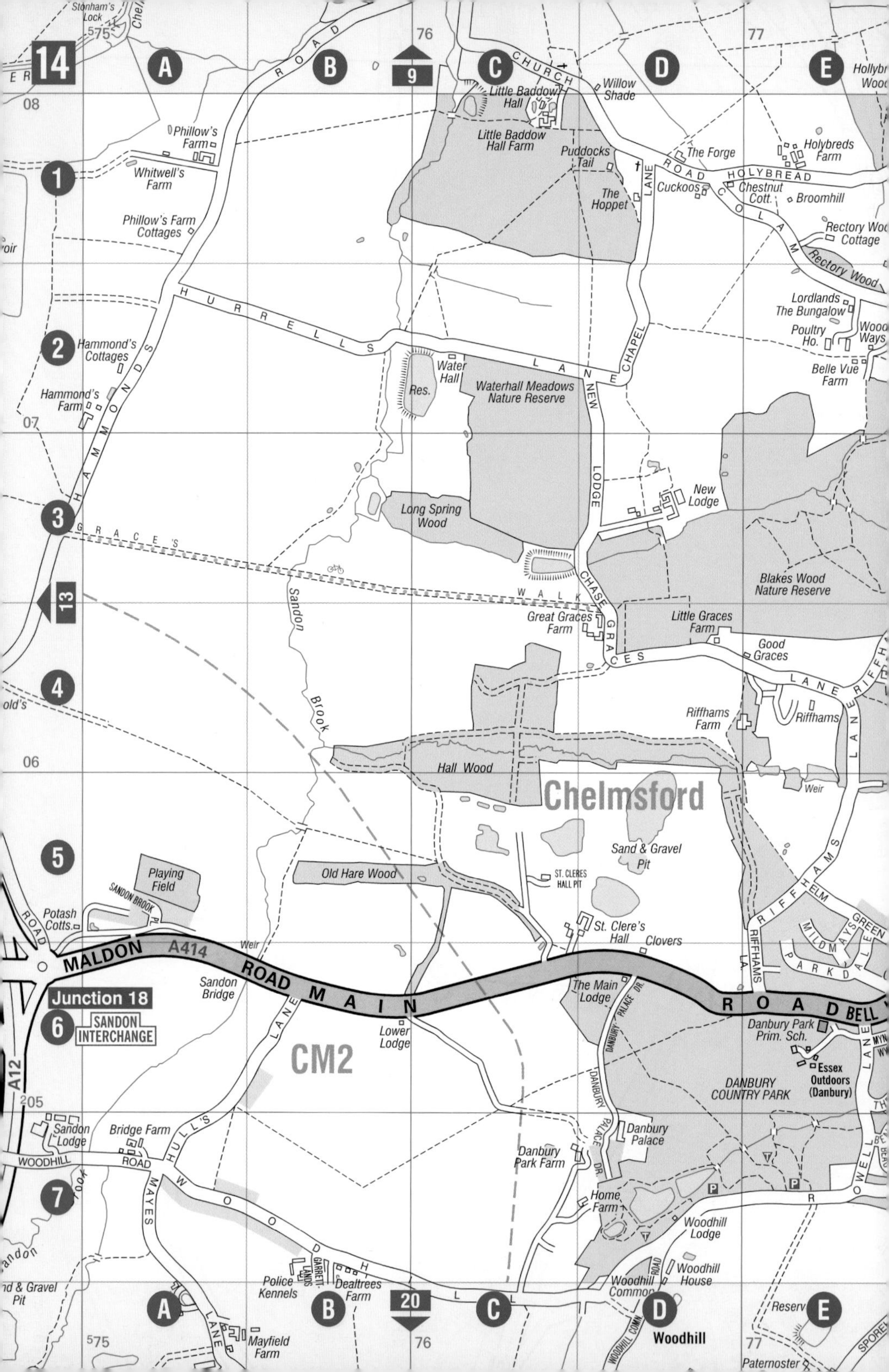

Stonham's Lock
Phillow's Farm
Whitwell's Farm
Phillow's Farm Cottages
Hammond's Cottages
Hammond's Farm
HAMMONDS ROAD
HURRELLS LANE
GRACES WALK
Little Baddow Hall
Little Baddow Hall Farm
CHURCH ROAD
Willow Shade
Puddocks Tail
The Hoppet
CHAPEL LANE
The Forge
Holybreds Farm
HOLYBREAD ROAD
Cuckoos
Chestnut Cott.
Broomhill
COLAM LANE
Rectory Wood Cottage
Rectory Wood
Lordlands
The Bungalow
Poultry Ho.
Belle Vue Farm
Water Hall
Res.
Waterhall Meadows Nature Reserve
NEW LODGE CHASE
New Lodge
Long Spring Wood
Blakes Wood Nature Reserve
Great Graces Farm
Little Graces Farm
Good Graces
GRACES LANE
Riffhams Farm
Riffhams
RIFFHAMS LANE
Sandon Brook
Hall Wood
Chelmsford
Weir
Sand & Gravel Pit
ST. CLERES HALL PIT
St. Clere's Hall
Clovers
Old Hare Wood
Playing Field
SANDON BROOK PL.
Potash Cotts.
MALDON ROAD A414
MAIN ROAD
BELL
Sandon Bridge
Junction 18
SANDON INTERCHANGE
A12
CM2
Lower Lodge
The Main Lodge
DANBURY PALACE DR.
RIFFHAMS CHASE
MILDMAYS
PARKDALE
GREEN
Danbury Park Prim. Sch.
Essex Outdoors (Danbury)
DANBURY COUNTRY PARK
Danbury Palace
Danbury Park Farm
Home Farm
Woodhill Lodge
Woodhill House
Woodhill Common
WOODHILL COMMON ROAD
Woodhill
Sandon Lodge
Bridge Farm
WOODHILL ROAD
HULL'S LANE
MAYES LANE
Police Kennels
GARRETT LANDS
Dealtrees Farm
Mayfield Farm
Sand & Gravel Pit
Paternoster
Reserv
76
77
08
07
06
205
575

9
13
20

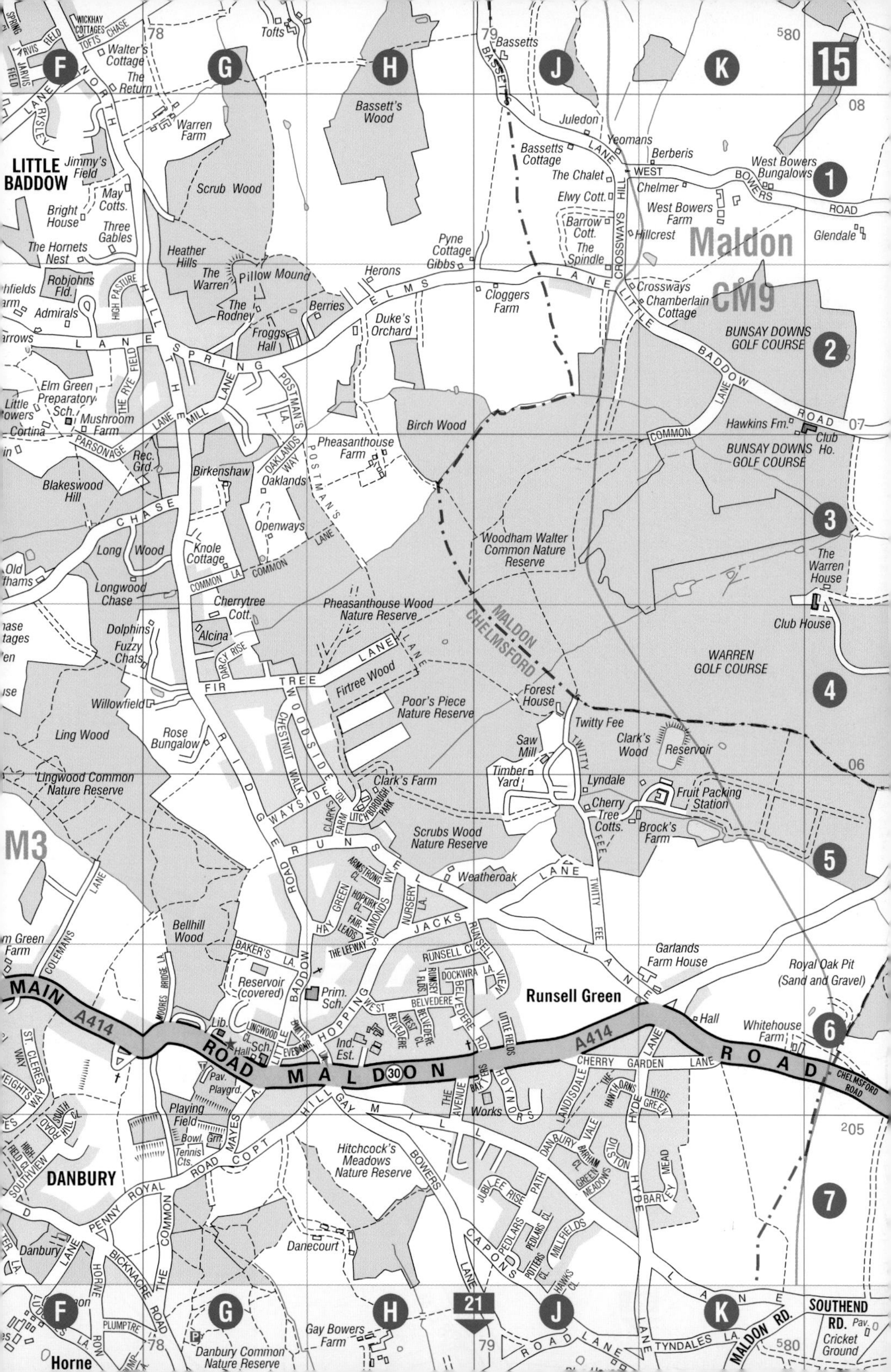
LITTLE BADDOW
Maldon
CM9
DANBURY
Runsell Green
Horne
Bassett's Wood
Scrub Wood
Birch Wood
Woodham Walter Common Nature Reserve
Pheasanthouse Wood Nature Reserve
Poor's Piece Nature Reserve
Scrubs Wood Nature Reserve
Lingwood Common Nature Reserve
Hitchcock's Meadows Nature Reserve
Danbury Common Nature Reserve
BUNSAY DOWNS GOLF COURSE
WARREN GOLF COURSE
MALDON
CHELMSFORD
MAIN ROAD
MALDON ROAD
A414
SOUTHEND RD.
21

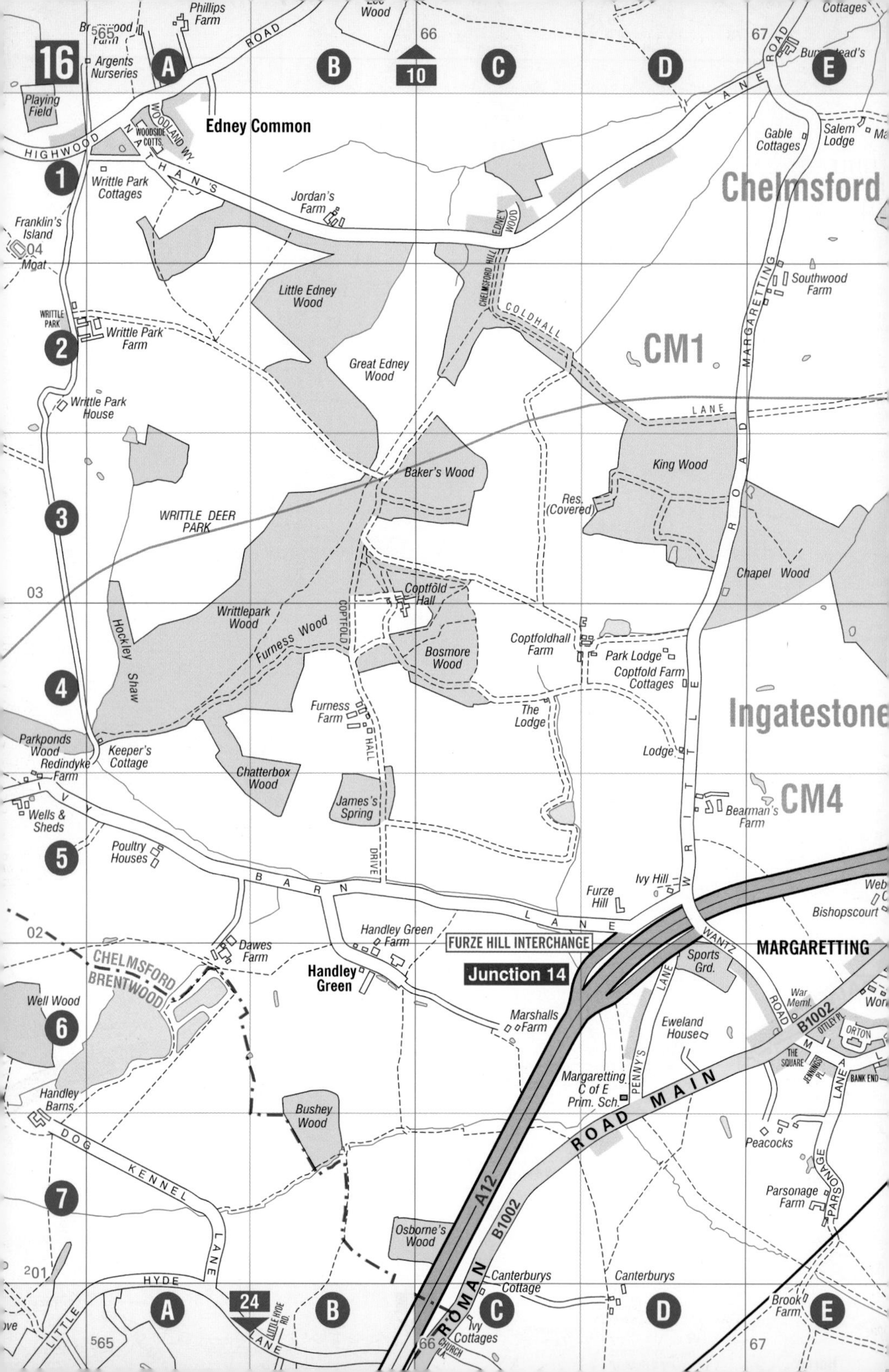
Phillips Farm
Argents Nurseries
Playing Field
Edney Common
WOODSIDE COTTS.
WOODLAND WY.
HIGHWOOD ROAD
NATHAN'S LANE
Writtle Park Cottages
Jordan's Farm
Franklin's Island
Moat
Gable Cottages
Salem Lodge
Chelmsford
EDNEY WOOD
CHELMSFORD HILL
COLDHALL LANE
Little Edney Wood
Southwood Farm
WRITTLE PARK
Writtle Park Farm
Great Edney Wood
CM1
Writtle Park House
MARGARETTING ROAD
King Wood
Baker's Wood
Res. (Covered)
WRITTLE DEER PARK
Chapel Wood
Coptfold Hall
COPTFOLD HALL DRIVE
Writtlepark Wood
Furness Wood
Hockley Shaw
Bosmore Wood
Coptfoldhall Farm
Park Lodge
Coptfold Farm Cottages
Ingatestone
Furness Farm
The Lodge
Parkponds Wood
Keeper's Cottage
Redindyke Farm
Chatterbox Wood
Lodge
WRITTLE ROAD
James's Spring
CM4
Bearman's Farm
Wells & Sheds
IVY BARN LANE
Poultry Houses
Ivy Hill
Furze Hill
Bishopscourt
FURZE HILL INTERCHANGE
Handley Green Farm
Dawes Farm
MARGARETTING
Junction 14
Handley Green
CHELMSFORD
BRENTWOOD
Sports Grd.
WANTZ ROAD
PENNY'S LANE
Well Wood
Marshalls Farm
Eweland House
War Meml.
B1002
OTTLEY PL.
ORTON
THE SQUARE
JENNINGS PL.
BANK END
Margaretting C of E Prim. Sch.
MAIN ROAD
Handley Barns
Bushey Wood
Peacocks
DOG KENNEL LANE
Parsonage Farm
PARSONAGE LANE
A12
Osborne's Wood
ROMAN ROAD
LITTLE HYDE LANE
LITTLE HYDE RD.
Canterburys Cottage
Canterburys
Brook Farm
Ivy Cottages
CHURCH LA.
Bumstead's
Cottages
A B C D E
1 2 3 4 5 6 7
565 66 67
04 03 02 01
10
24

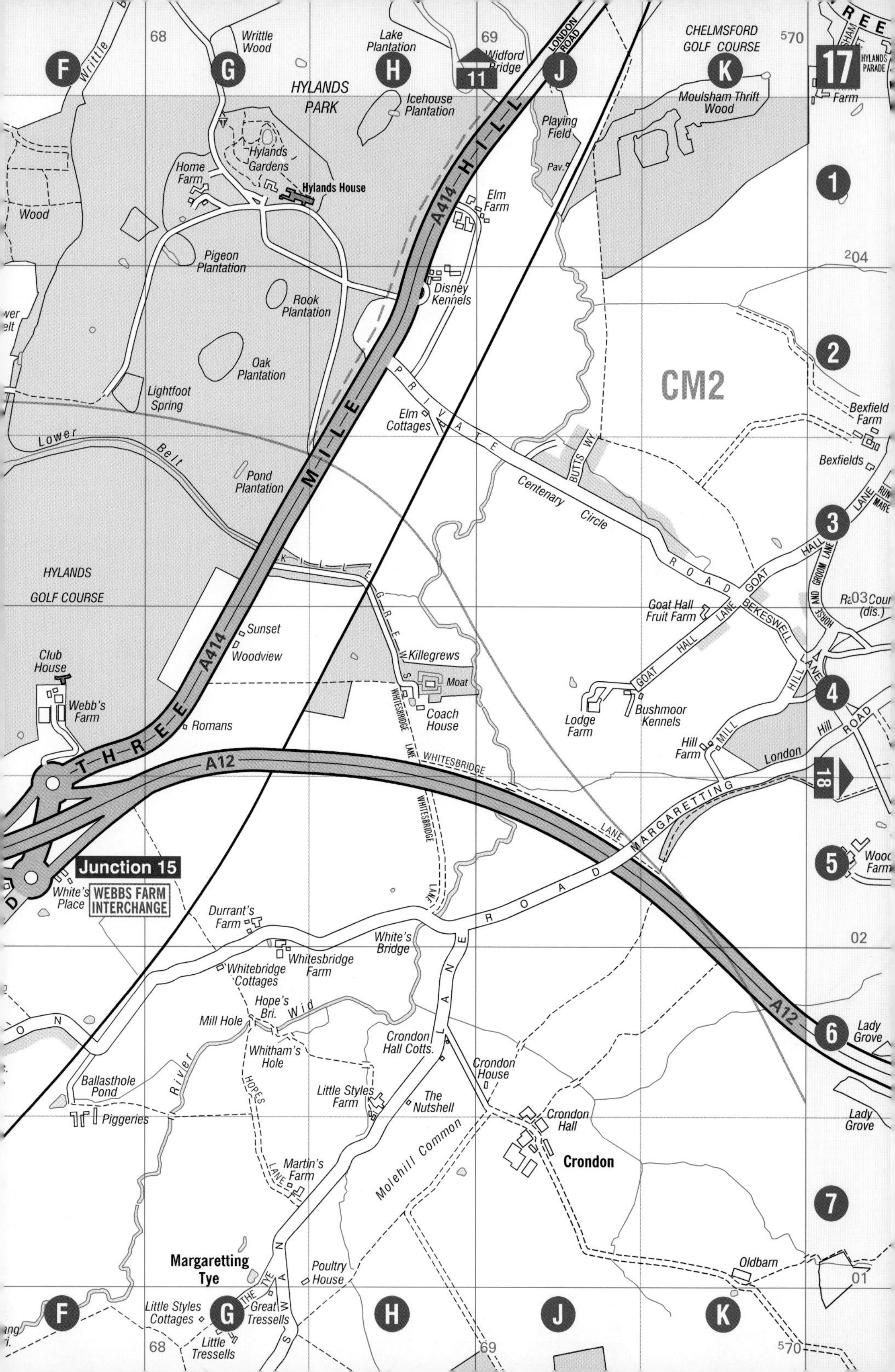
17
Writtle Wood
Lake Plantation
Widford Bridge
11
LONDON ROAD
CHELMSFORD GOLF COURSE
HYLANDS PARADE
Farm
HYLANDS PARK
Icehouse Plantation
Moulsham Thrift Wood
Playing Field
Pav.
Hylands Gardens
Home Farm
Hylands House
Elm Farm
Wood
Pigeon Plantation
Disney Kennels
Rook Plantation
Oak Plantation
CM2
Lightfoot Spring
PRIVATE
Elm Cottages
BUTTS WY.
Bexfield Farm
Bexfields
Lower Belt
Pond Plantation
Centenary Circle
THREE MILE HILL
A414
HYLANDS GOLF COURSE
KILLEGREWS
ROAD
GOAT HALL LANE
Goat Hall Fruit Farm
BEKESWELL LANE
HORSE AND GROOM LANE
Sunset
Woodview
Killegrews
Moat
Club House
Webb's Farm
Coach House
Romans
WHITESBRIDGE LANE
Lodge Farm
Bushmoor Kennels
Hill Farm
MILL
HILL
Hill Road
London Road
A12
18
MARGARETTING ROAD
Junction 15
White's Place
WEBBS FARM INTERCHANGE
Wood Farm
Durrant's Farm
White's Bridge
Whitebridge Cottages
Whitesbridge Farm
Hope's Bri.
Wid
Mill Hole
LANE
Crondon Hall Cotts.
Lady Grove
Whitham's Hole
River
HOPES LANE
Crondon House
Ballasthole Pond
Little Styles Farm
The Nutshell
Piggeries
Crondon Hall
Molehill Common
Crondon
Martin's Farm
Margaretting Tye
Poultry House
Oldbarn
SWAN LANE
THE TYE
Little Styles Cottages
Great Tressells
Little Tressells
F
G
H
J
K
1
2
3
4
5
6
7
68
69
570
204
03
02
01

GREAT BADDOW
Chelmsford
CM2
GALLEYWOOD
Galleyend
Great Baddow High Sch.
Beehive Lane Prim. School
Mildmay Jun. & Infs. Schs.
Prim. & Nursery Schs.
Thrift Farm
Lathcoats Farm
Nursery
Hall
Playing Field
Appletrees
Riding School
Carlton House
Chelmer Park
Playground
Pavilion
Sports Ground
Oak Nursery
Great Seabrights
Deadman's Well
Bexfield Farm
Bexfields
Thriftwood Sch.
Vic.
White House
Race Course (dis.)
Res. (covered)
Lib.
Jun.& Inf. Schs.
Reservoir
Canon-Leys Farm
Parklands Farm
Baddow Park Farmhouse
GALLEYWOOD COMMON
Wood Farm
Byron Hall
Pond's Farm
Glebe Farm Cottages
Lady Grove
The Chase
GALLEYWOOD/STOCK INTERCHANGE
Junction 16
Works
Gay Bowers Farm
Temple Grove
TEMPLE GROVE CARAVAN PARK
Long Leys
TEMPLETON PARK
Depot
TEMPLE FARM TRADING ESTATE
Little Peverels
The Red House
Tanfield Tye Cottages
Oldbarn
Temple Wood
A12
B1007
B1009
GALLEYWOOD ROAD
STOCK ROAD
BEEHIVE LANE
GOSHAWK DRIVE
DEADMAN'S LANE
GALLEYWOOD ROAD
BROOK LANE
SLADE'S LANE
GOAT HALL LANE
HORSE AND GROOM LANE
BEKESWELL LANE
MARGARETTING ROAD
WATCHOUSE ROAD
PYMS ROAD
GREEN RIGNALS
LOWER ROAD
BARNARD ROAD
PONDS ROAD
WELL LANE
BAKERS LANE
WEST HANNINGFIELD ROAD
12
17
London
A
B
C
D
E
1
2
3
4
5
6
7

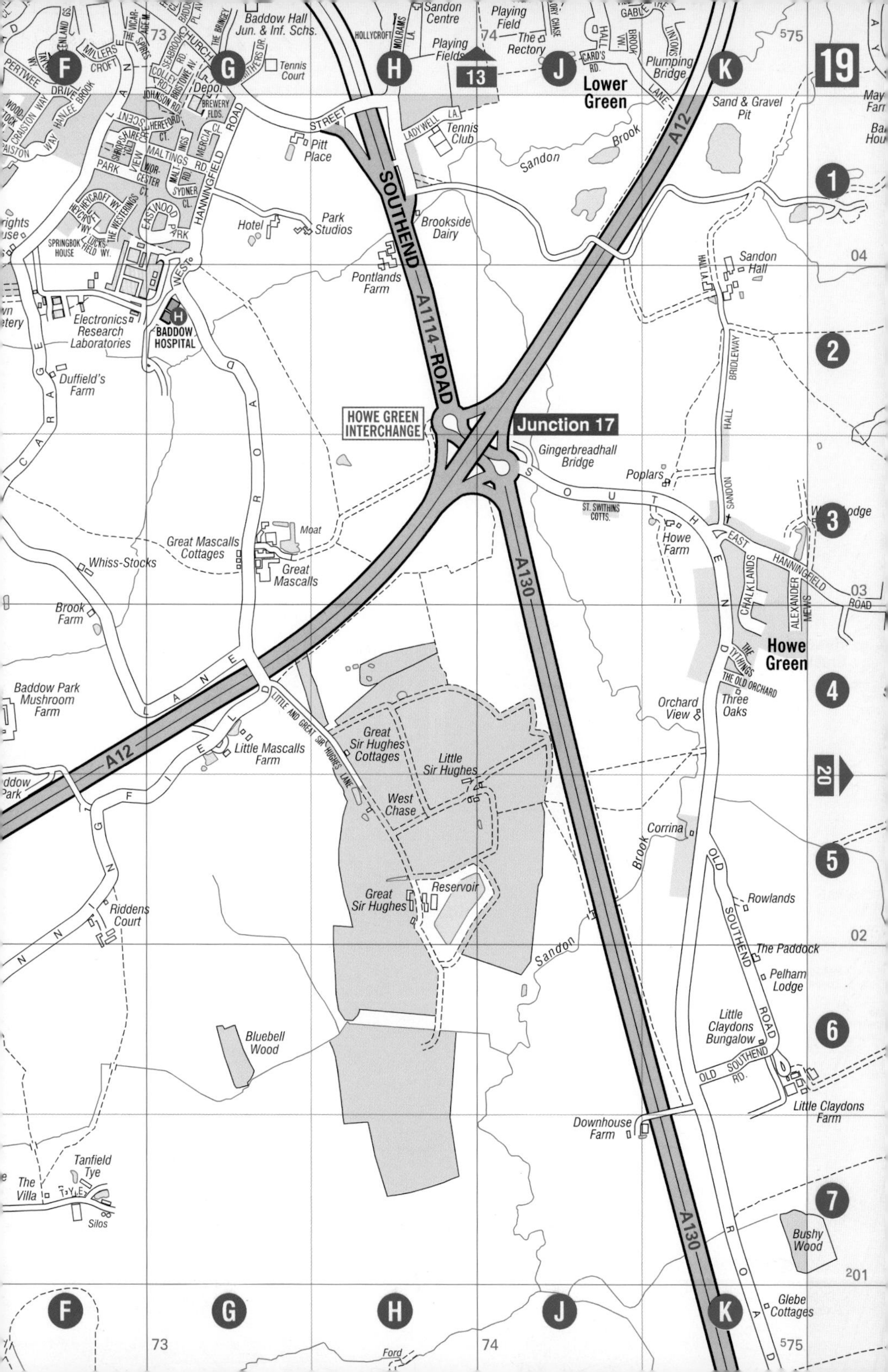

Baddow Hall Jun. & Inf. Schs.
Sandon Centre
Playing Field
The Rectory
Playing Fields
13
Lower Green
Plumping Bridge
Sand & Gravel Pit
Tennis Court
Depot
Pitt Place
Tennis Club
Sandon Brook
Hotel
Park Studios
Brookside Dairy
Pontlands Farm
Sandon Hall
Electronics Research Laboratories
BADDOW HOSPITAL
Duffield's Farm
SOUTHEND A1114 ROAD
A12
A130
HOWE GREEN INTERCHANGE
Junction 17
Gingerbreadhall Bridge
Poplars
ST. SWITHINS COTTS.
Howe Farm
Moat
Great Mascalls Cottages
Great Mascalls
Whiss-Stocks
Brook Farm
Baddow Park Mushroom Farm
Howe Green
EAST HANNINGFIELD ROAD
CHALKLANDS
ALEXANDER MEWS
THE TYTHINGS
THE OLD ORCHARD
Three Oaks
Orchard View
Little Mascalls Farm
LITTLE AND GREAT SIR HUGHES LANE
Great Sir Hughes Cottages
Little Sir Hughes
West Chase
20
Corrina
Brook
Reservoir
Great Sir Hughes
Riddens Court
Rowlands
OLD SOUTHEND ROAD
The Paddock
Pelham Lodge
Little Claydons Bungalow
Little Claydons Farm
Sandon
Bluebell Wood
Downhouse Farm
Tanfield Tye
The Villa
Silos
Bushy Wood
Glebe Cottages
Ford
SPRINGBOK HOUSE
HANNINGFIELD ROAD
VICARAGE LANE
GALLEYWOOD ROAD
WEST HANNINGFIELD ROAD
BRIDLEWAY
SANDON HALL LA.
LADY WELL LA.
STREET
HOLLYCROFT
MOLRAMS LA.
CARD'S RD.
F G H J K
1 2 3 4 5 6 7
73 74 575
04 03 02 201

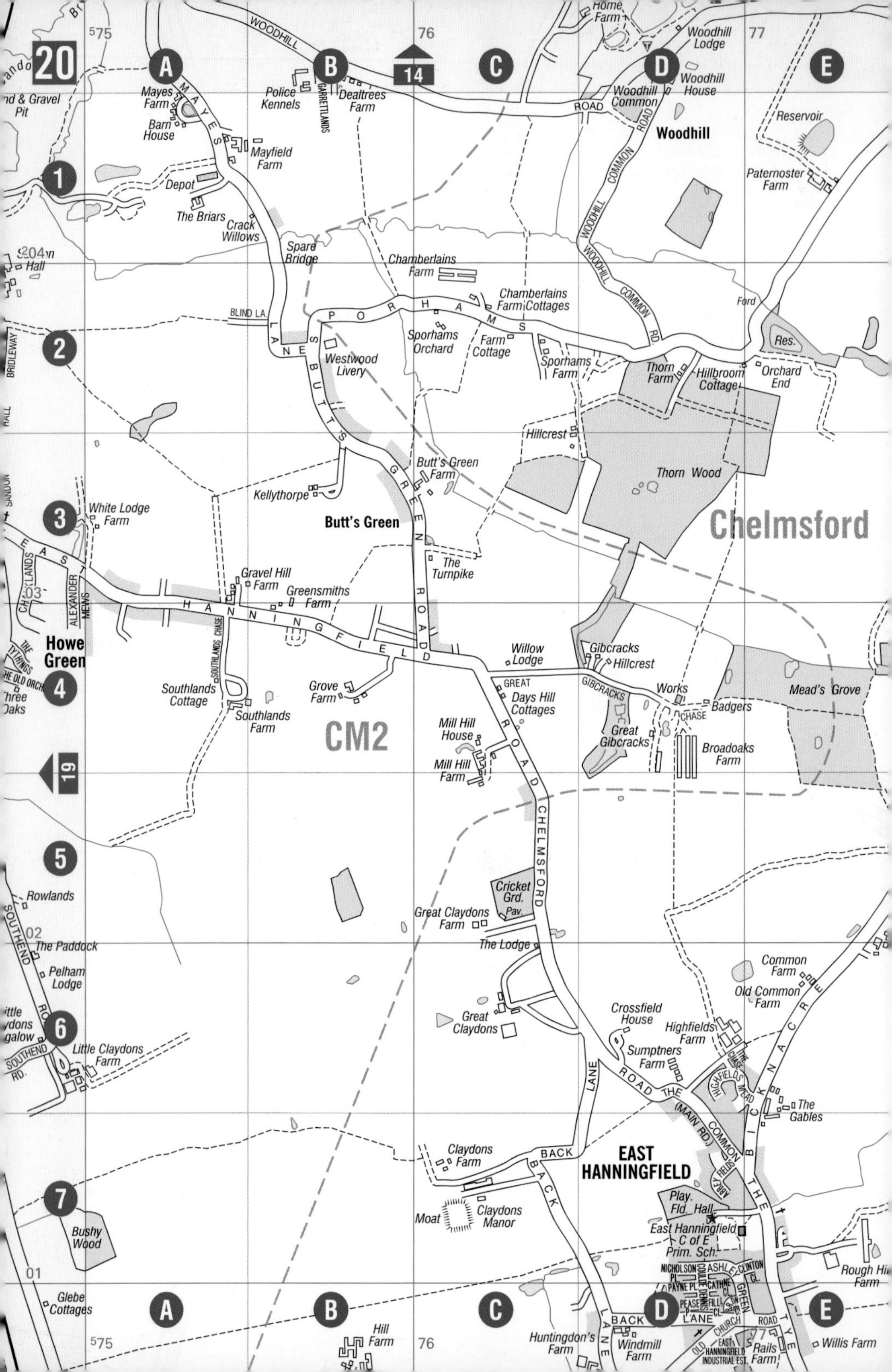
A
B
C
D
E
1
2
3
4
5
6
7
575
76
77
14
19
Woodhill Road
Mayes Farm
Barn House
Mayes Lane
Police Kennels
Garrettlands
Dealtrees Farm
Home Farm
Woodhill Lodge
Woodhill House
Woodhill Common
Woodhill
Woodhill Common Road
Reservoir
Paternoster Farm
Sand & Gravel Pit
Mayfield Farm
Depot
The Briars
Crack Willows
Spare Bridge
Chamberlains Farm
Chamberlains Farm Cottages
Blind La.
Sporhams Lane
Sporhams Orchard
Farm Cottage
Sporhams Farm
Westwood Livery
Butts Green Road
Thorn Farm
Hillbroom Cottage
Orchard End
Res.
Ford
Bridleway
Hillcrest
Thorn Wood
Butt's Green Farm
Kellythorpe
White Lodge Farm
Butt's Green
Chelmsford
East Hanningfield Road
Chalklands
Alexander Mews
Howe Green
The Tythings
The Old Orchard
Three Oaks
Gravel Hill Farm
Greensmiths Farm
The Turnpike
Southlands Chase
Willow Lodge
Gibcracks
Hillcrest
Great Gibcracks Chase
Works
Badgers
Mead's Grove
Southlands Cottage
Southlands Farm
Grove Farm
Days Hill Cottages
Great Gibcracks
Broadoaks Farm
CM2
Mill Hill House
Mill Hill Farm
Chelmsford Road
Rowlands
Southend Road
The Paddock
Pelham Lodge
Cricket Grd.
Pav.
Great Claydons Farm
The Lodge
Common Farm
Old Common Farm
Great Claydons
Crossfield House
Highfields Farm
Sumptners Farm
Little Claydons Farm
Highfields Mead
The Chase
Bicknacre Road
The Common (Main Rd.)
The Gables
Claydons Farm
Back Lane
East Hanningfield
Abbey Fields
Play. Fld.
Hall
Moat
Claydons Manor
Bushy Wood
East Hanningfield C of E Prim. Sch.
Nicholson Pl.
Payne Pl.
Ashley Green
Clinton Cl.
Rough Hill Farm
Glebe Cottages
Hill Farm
Huntingdon's Farm
Windmill Farm
Old Church Lane
East Hanningfield Industrial Est.
Rails Farm
The Tye
Willis Farm

Horne Row
Reservoir
Danbury Common Nature Reserve
Backwarden Nature Reserve
Ball's Farm
Gay Bowers Farm
Danecourt
Gay Bowers
Manor Farm
Blue House Farm
Reservoirs
Poplar Farm
Overshot Bri.
Overshot Farm
Springate Farm
Peartree Farm
Little Gibcracks
Compasses Farm
Priory Prim. Sch.
Cemetery
CM3
Saint Giles
Remains of Priory (Augustinian founded 1175)
Horseshoe Farm
Horseshoe Nurseries
BICKNACRE
The Old Convent Moor House
South Gibcracks
Playing Field
Folks Wood
Thrift Wood Nature Reserve
Leigham's Farm
Leighams
Woodham Hall
Moat
Niagara
The Spinney
Foxes Close
Hounds Hill Farm
Reservoir
Chalk Bridge
The Hyde
Hyde Farm Nursery
Slough House Wood
Old Chase Farm
Eves Farm
White Elm Farm
Jacklett's Farm
Jacklett's Wood
New England Wood
Maldon
CM9
Cricket Grd.
Pav.
GAY BOWERS ROAD
WHITE ELM ROAD
MALDON ROAD
HYDE LANE
MAIN ROAD
PRIORY ROAD
SLOUGH ROAD
TYNDALES LA.
LEIGHAMS
B1418
CROWS LANE
15
F
G
H
J
K
1
2
3
4
5
6
7

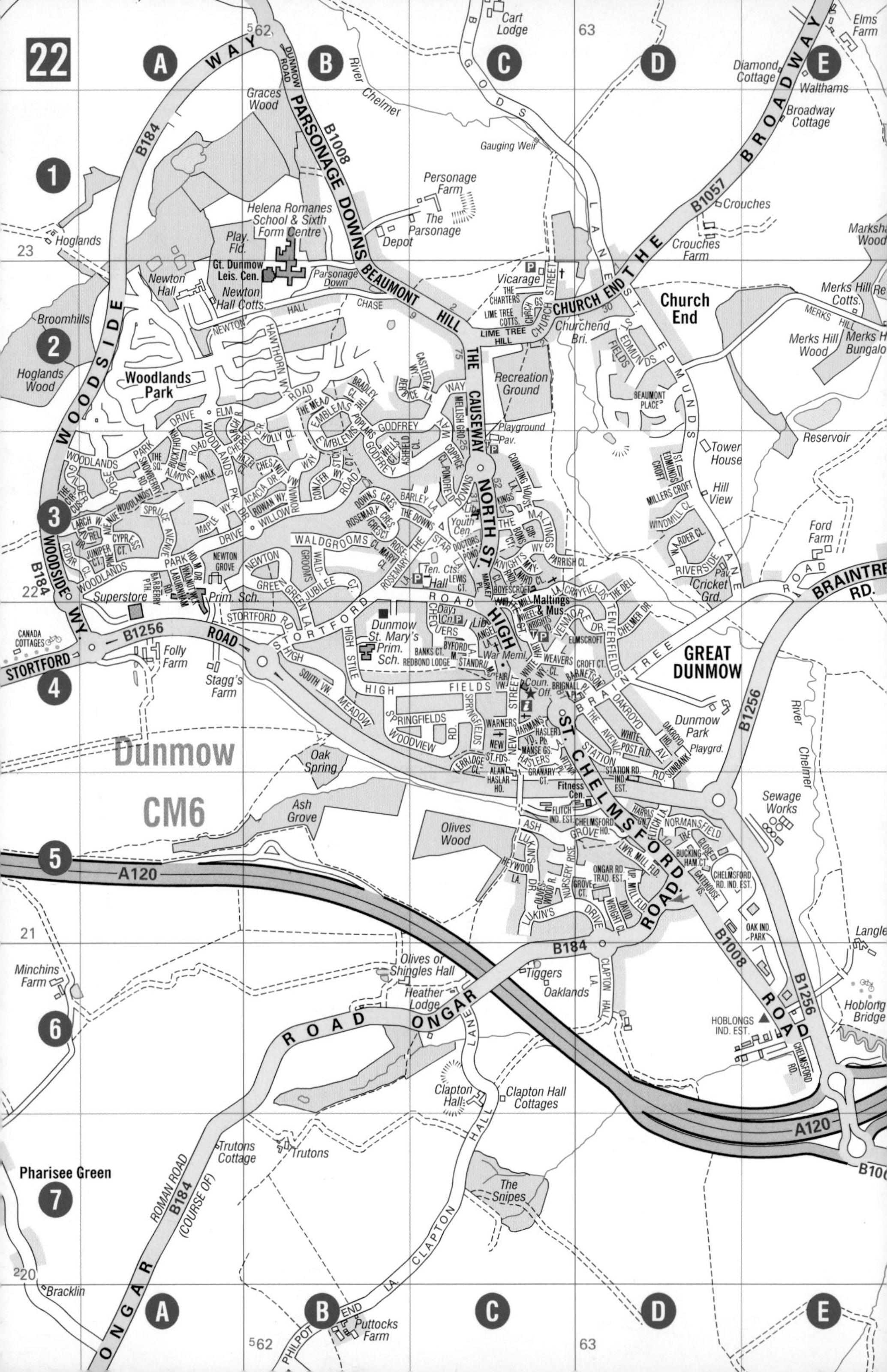

Dunmow
CM6
GREAT DUNMOW
Church End
Woodlands Park
Pharisee Green
Helena Romanes School & Sixth Form Centre
Gt. Dunmow Leis. Cen.
Newton Hall
Recreation Ground
Maltings & Mus.
Dunmow St. Mary's Prim. Sch.
Superstore
Dunmow Park
Sewage Works
Olives Wood
Oak Spring
Ash Grove
Clapton Hall
The Snipes
Puttocks Farm
Hoblongs Ind. Est.

23
F
G
H
J
K
1
2
3
4
5
6
7
81
82
83
16
15
14
13
Witham
CM8
RIVENHALL OAKS
GOLF CENTRE
Burghey Brook
Poultry Farm
Club Ho.
Southview
School
New
Rickstones
Academy
Elm Hall
Prim. Sch.
New
Cottages
Glebe
Farm
The Old
Rectory
Lodge
Warren
Farm
CRESSING ROAD
B1018
Templars
Prim. Sch.
RECTORY LANE
FOREST ROAD
RICKSTONES ROAD
Recreation
Ground
Cemy.
CYPRESS ROAD
Superstore
COLEMAN'S
INTERCHANGE
Junc
22
COLEMANS BRIDGE
LONDON RD.
A12
EASTWAYS
WATERSIDE
BUS. PK.
Works
Factory
Depot
FREEBOURNES
FREEBOURNES
RD. IND. EST.
SWAN VALE
INDUSTRIAL
ESTATE
Factories
Works
STEPFIELD
WHEATON RD.
Factory
Works
Depot
Capitol
Square
WHEATEAR
IND. EST.
BRIARSFORD
WITHAM
IND. EST.
Sewage
Works
Lagoon
Sub.
Chipping
Hill
Bramston
Green
Comm.
Cen.
Vicarage
Hall
Chipping
Hill Bridge
Powers Hall
End
POWERS HALL END
Subway
Victoria
Cottages
Powers Hall
Academy
Powers Hall
Inf. Sch.
HONEYSUCKLE
FLORA
CORNEL CL.
BRYONY CL.
SPEEDWELL
CL.
CALAMINT
FOXGLOVE
CL.
SAMPHIRE
CL.
ROSEBAY
TERLING ROAD
Witham
BRAINTREE RD.
COLLINGWOOD RD.
NEWLAND ST.
MALDON RD.
COLCHESTER ROAD
B1389
WITHAM
Govt.
Offices
Catholic
Bridge
THE AVENUE
THE PADDOCKS
Dorothy L
Sayers
Cen.
THE NEWLANDS
SHOPPING
CEN.
THE
GROVE CEN.
Comm.
Cen.
Rec.
Grd.
Sports
Ground
Tennis
Courts
CHELMER ROAD
ARMOND
GUITHAVON ROAD
Witham Town
FC
Club
House
Club
House
Football
Ground
Playing
Field
Blunt's Hall
Farm
BLUNTS HALL DR.
Blunt's
Hall
Moat
Maltings
Academy
Witham
Leisure Cen.
Witham
Bridge
Bramston
Sports Ground
STEVENS RD.
Pavs.
BRIDGE ROAD
Saul's
Bridge
RIVER VW.
BLACKWATER LANE
LAURENCE AVENUE
Playing
Field
Schs.
MALTINGS LANE
Jackson's
Farm
Sch.
Prim.
Sch.
Superstore
Sports
Fld.
HATFIELD ROAD
B1389
Lodge
Farm
Lodge Farm
Cottages
WITHAM STH.
INTERCHANGE
Junc. 21
Nursy. Sch.
BOULEVARD
Home
Fm.
Dengie
Farm
HOWBRIDGE
HALL RD.
Subway
BLUE MILLS HILL
Benton
Hall
Blue
Mills
Blue Mills
Bridge
R. Blackwater
BENTON HALL
GOLF COURSE
Club
House
Reservoir
MALDON ROAD
B1018
BRAINTREE
MALDON

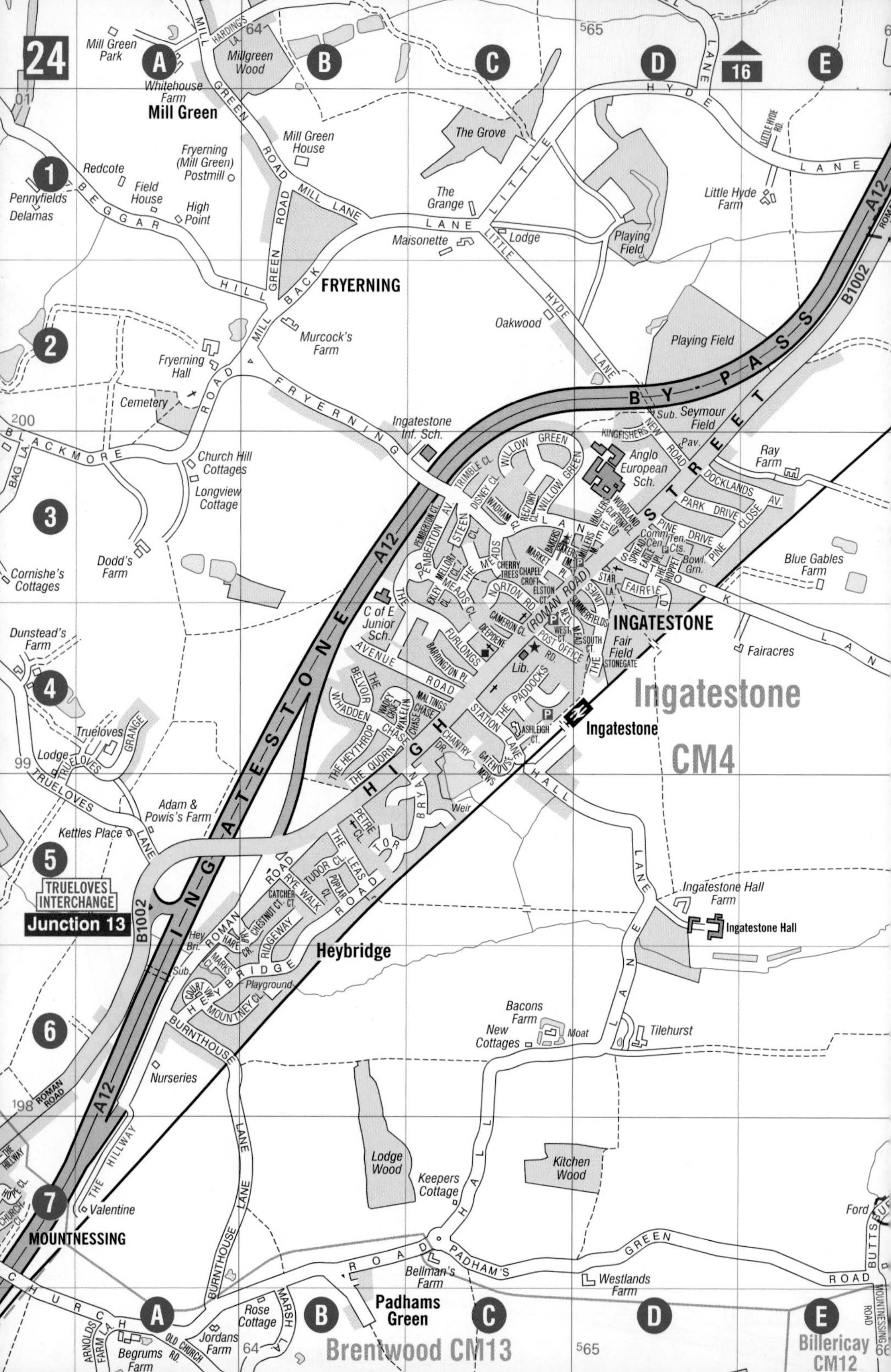
Mill Green Park
Whitehouse Farm
Mill Green
Millgreen Wood
Mill Green House
Fryerning (Mill Green) Postmill
Redcote
Field House
High Point
Pennyfields
Delamas
The Grove
The Grange
Maisonette
Lodge
Playing Field
Little Hyde Farm
FRYERNING
Murcock's Farm
Fryerning Hall
Cemetery
Oakwood
Playing Field
Seymour Field
Ingatestone Inf. Sch.
Church Hill Cottages
Longview Cottage
Dodd's Farm
Cornishe's Cottages
Anglo European Sch.
Ray Farm
Blue Gables Farm
C of E Junior Sch.
INGATESTONE
Fair Field
Fairacres
Dunstead's Farm
Trueloves
Lodge
Ingatestone
Ingatestone CM4
Adam & Powis's Farm
Kettles Place
TRUELOVES INTERCHANGE
Junction 13
Weir
Ingatestone Hall Farm
Ingatestone Hall
Heybridge
Playground
Bacons Farm
New Cottages
Moat
Tilehurst
Nurseries
Lodge Wood
Keepers Cottage
Kitchen Wood
Valentine
MOUNTNESSING
Ford
Bellman's Farm
Westlands Farm
Rose Cottage
Padhams Green
Jordans Farm
Begrums Farm
Brentwood CM13
Billericay CM12
INGATESTONE BY-PASS
HIGH STREET
A12
B1002
16

Maldon
CM9
MALDON
HEYBRIDGE
Heybridge Wood
Grapnell's Farm
Old Rectory
Langford Place
Elms Farm
Chelmer Ho.
MALDON GOLF COURSE
Club House
Chelmer and Blackwater Navigation
River Blackwater
Heybridge Creek
Superstore
Timber Yard
Combined Military Services Mus.
Blackwater Trading Estate
Hospice
Heybridge Cen.
Cemetery
Hall Bridge
Middle Farm
Heybridge Prim. Sch.
Heybridge Swifts FC
Pavilion
Lofts
Thomas Plume's Lib.
St. Peter's Hospital
Plume Sch.
Playing Fields
Council Offs.
Maldon Prim. Sch.
Maldon District Museum
Maldon Yacht Club
The Hythe
Marine Lake
Boating Lake
Promenade Park
Rec. Grd. & Marine Parade
Park Drive Health Club
Blackwater Leisure Centre
Madison Heights
Maldon & Tiptree FC (Wallace Binder Ground)
South House Farm
St. Giles Leper Hosp. (ruins)
Wentworth Prim. Sch.
Wintersleet Farm
West Station Ind. Est.
A414
B1018
B1022
B1026
LANGFORD RD.
HEYBRIDGE APPROACH
THE CAUSEWAY
COLCHESTER RD.
GOLDHANGER ROAD
BROAD STREET GREEN ROAD
SPITAL R.
LIMEBROOK WAY
MUNDON ROAD
PARK DRIVE
F G H J K
1 2 3 4 5 6 7
585
86
09
08
207
06

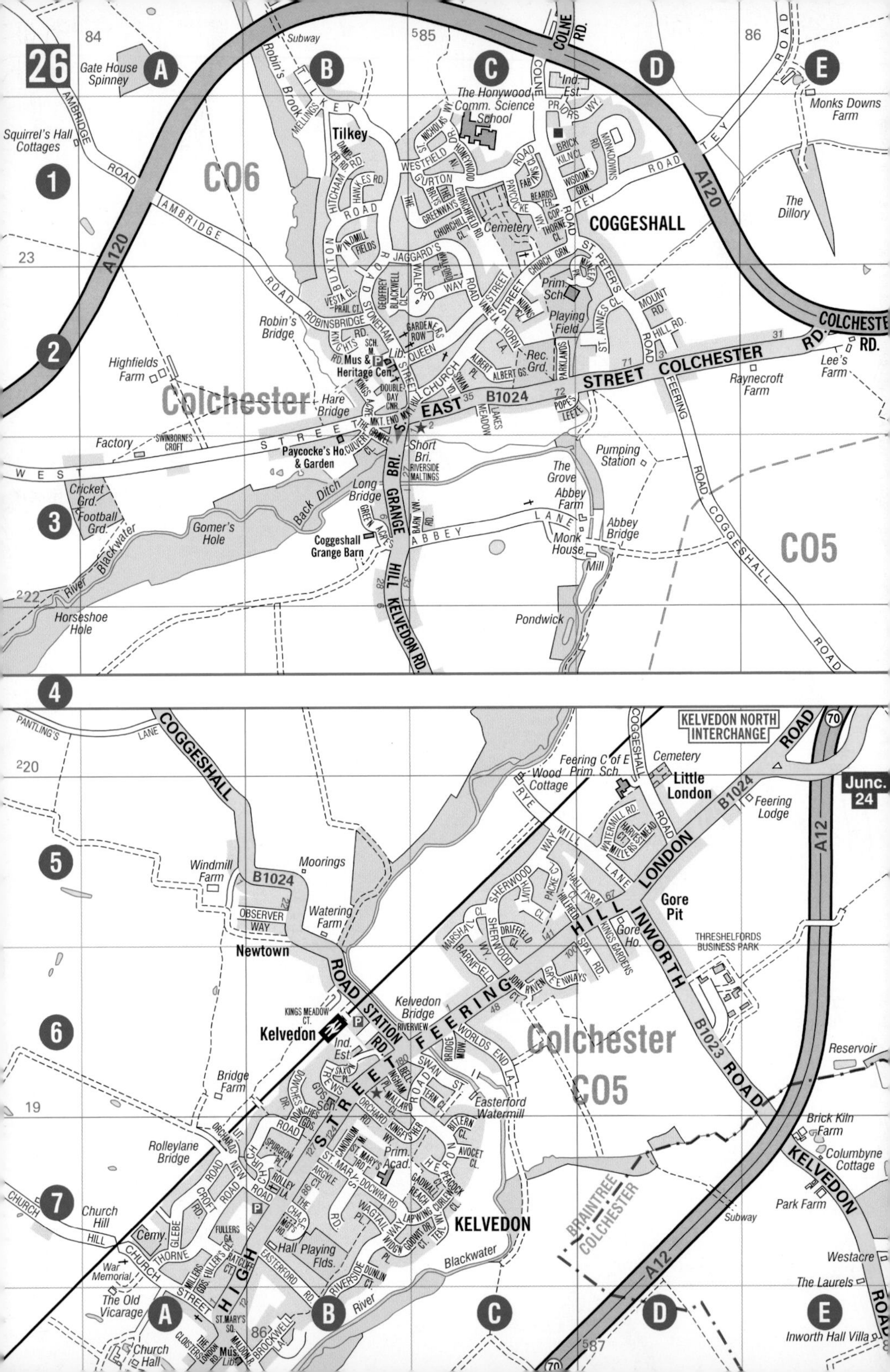

Gate House Spinney
Squirrel's Hall Cottages
Subway
Robin's Brook
Tilkey
The Honywood Comm. Science School
Ind. Est.
Monks Downs Farm
CO6
COGGESHALL
The Dillory
Cemetery
Prim. Sch.
Playing Field
Rec. Grd.
Robin's Bridge
Highfields Farm
Mus & Heritage Cen.
Lib.
Colchester
Hare Bridge
EAST STREET COLCHESTER RD.
B1024
Raynecroft Farm
Lee's Farm
Factory
Paycocke's Ho. & Garden
Short Bri.
Pumping Station
The Grove
Cricket Grd.
Football Grd.
Gomer's Hole
Back Ditch
Long Bridge
Abbey Farm
Abbey Bridge
Coggeshall Grange Barn
Monk House
Mill
CO5
River Blackwater
Horseshoe Hole
Pondwick
GRANGE HILL KELVEDON RD.
A120
KELVEDON NORTH INTERCHANGE
Cemetery
Feering C of E Prim. Sch.
Wood Cottage
Little London
Feering Lodge
Junc. 24
A12
Windmill Farm
Moorings
Watering Farm
Newtown
Gore Pit
Gore Ho.
THRESHELFORDS BUSINESS PARK
Kelvedon Bridge
Kelvedon
Ind. Est.
Colchester
CO5
Reservoir
Bridge Farm
Easterford Watermill
Brick Kiln Farm
Rolleylane Bridge
Prim. Acad.
Columbyne Cottage
Church Hill
Park Farm
KELVEDON
BRAINTREE
COLCHESTER
Subway
Cemy.
Hall Playing Flds.
Blackwater
War Memorial
Westacre
The Laurels
The Old Vicarage
River
Inworth Hall Villa
Church Hall
Mus. Lib.

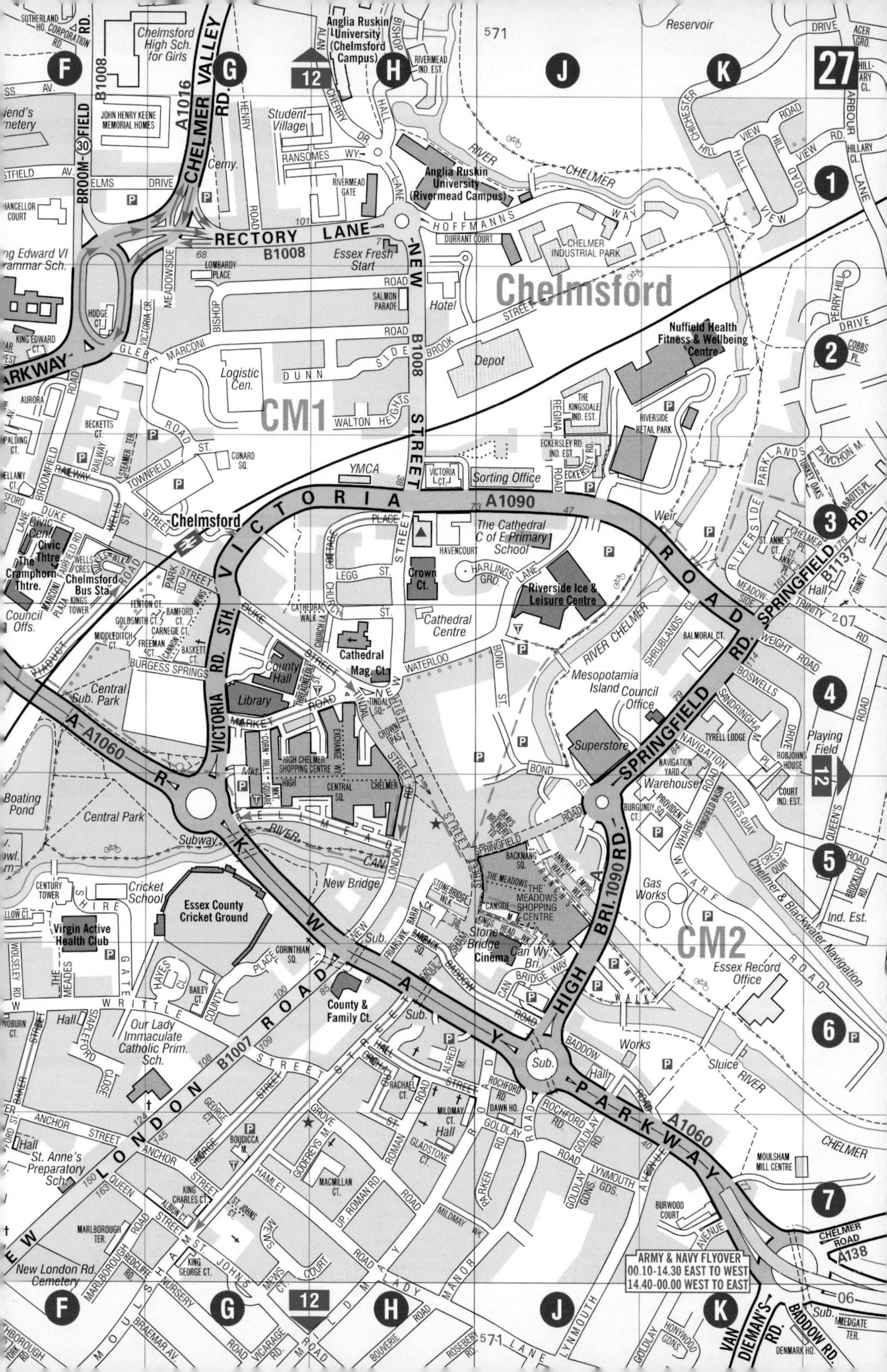
27
Chelmsford
CM1
CM2
Anglia Ruskin University (Chelmsford Campus)
Anglia Ruskin University (Rivermead Campus)
Chelmsford High Sch. for Girls
John Henry Keene Memorial Homes
Student Village
Rivermead Ind. Est.
Reservoir
Rectory Lane
B1008
A1016
Chelmer Valley Rd.
Broomfield
Parkway
A1060
Hoffmanns Way
Chelmer Industrial Park
Durrant Court
Essex Fresh Start
Hotel
Depot
Logistic Cen.
Nuffield Health Fitness & Wellbeing Centre
The Kingsdale Ind. Est.
Riverside Retail Park
Eckersley Rd. Ind. Est.
Sorting Office
YMCA
Victoria Ct.
Victoria Road
A1090
Chelmsford
The Cathedral C of E Primary School
Crown Ct.
Cathedral Centre
Cathedral Mag. Ct.
Riverside Ice & Leisure Centre
Civic Cen.
Civic Thtre.
The Cramphorn Thtre.
Chelmsford Bus Sta.
Council Offs.
County Hall
Library
High Chelmer Shopping Centre
Central Sq.
Mkt.
Central Sub. Park
Central Park
Boating Pond
Subway
New Bridge
Cricket School
Essex County Cricket Ground
Virgin Active Health Club
Mesopotamia Island
Council Office
Superstore
Springfield Rd.
Navigation Yard
Warehouse
Tyrell Lodge
Playing Field
Court Ind. Est.
Gas Works
Chelmer & Blackwater Navigation
Ind. Est.
Essex Record Office
The Meadows Shopping Centre
Stone Bridge
Cinema
Can Wy. Bri.
High Bri. 1090 Rd.
County & Family Ct.
Our Lady Immaculate Catholic Prim. Sch.
London Road B1007
St. Anne's Preparatory Sch.
New London Rd. Cemetery
Works
Sluice
River Chelmer
Moulsham Mill Centre
Burwood Court
Army & Navy Flyover
00.10-14.30 East to West
14.40-00.00 West to East
Van Dieman's Rd.
Baddow Rd.
Chelmer Road
A138
Moulsham St.
Mildmay Rd.
Lady Lane
12
F
G
H
J
K
1
2
3
4
5
6
7
571

INDEX

Including Streets, Places & Areas, Hospitals etc., Industrial Estates,
Selected Flats & Walkways, Junction Names, Stations and Selected Places of Interest.

HOW TO USE THIS INDEX

1. Each street name is followed by its Postcode District, then by its Locality abbreviation(s) and then by its map reference; e.g. **Abbey La.** CO6: Cogg . . . .3C **26** is in the CO6 Postcode District and the Coggeshall Locality and is to be found in square 3C on page **26**. The page number is shown in bold type.

2. A strict alphabetical order is followed in which Av., Rd., St., etc. (though abbreviated) are read in full and as part of the street name; e.g. **Ashby Rd.** appears after **Ash Bungs.** but before **Ash Cl.**

3. Streets and a selection of flats and walkways that cannot be shown on the mapping, appear in the index with the thoroughfare to which they are connected shown in brackets; e.g. **Augustus M.** *CM7: Brain . . . .5E* **4** *(off Pierrefitte Way)*

4. Addresses that are in more than one part are referred to as not continuous.

5. Places and areas are shown in the index in **BLUE TYPE** and the map reference is to the actual map square in which the town centre or area is located and not to the place name shown on the map; e.g. **BOCKING 2F 5**

6. An example of a selected place of interest is **Braintree District Mus. 4F 5**

7. Examples of stations are:
Braintree Freeport Station (Rail) . . . .6H 5; Braintree Bus Station . . . .4F 5; Maldon (Park & Ride) 3H 25

8. Junction names are shown in the index in **BOLD CAPITAL TYPE**; e.g. **BOREHAM INTERCHANGE 5D 8**

9. An example of a Hospital, Hospice or selected Healthcare facility is **BADDOW HOSPITAL 2G 19**

10. Map references for entries that appear on large scale page **27** are shown first, with small scale map references shown in brackets; e.g. **Albion Ct.** CM2: Chelm 7G **27** (4B **12**)

GENERAL ABBREVIATIONS

App. : Approach
Av. : Avenue
Blvd. : Boulevard
Bri. : Bridge
Bungs. : Bungalows
Bus. : Business
Cvn. : Caravan
Cen. : Centre
Cl. : Close
Comn. : Common
Cnr. : Corner
Cotts. : Cottages
Ct. : Court
Cres. : Crescent
Cft. : Croft
Dr. : Drive
E. : East
Ent. : Enterprise
Est. : Estate
Fld. : Field
Flds. : Fields
Gdn. : Garden
Gdns. : Gardens
Ga. : Gate
Gt. : Great
Grn. : Green
Gro. : Grove
Hgts. : Heights
Ho. : House
Ind. : Industrial
Info. : Information
La. : Lane
Lit. : Little
Lwr. : Lower
Mnr. : Manor
Mdw. : Meadow
Mdws. : Meadows
M. : Mews
Mt. : Mount
Mus. : Museum
Nth. : North
Pde. : Parade
Pk. : Park
Pas. : Passage
Pl. : Place
Ri. : Rise
Rd. : Road
Rdbt. : Roundabout
Shop. : Shopping
Sth. : South
Sq. : Square
St. : Street
Ter. : Terrace
Twr. : Tower
Trad. : Trading
Up. : Upper
Va. : Vale
Vw. : View
Vs. : Villas
Wlk. : Walk
W. : West
Yd. : Yard

LOCALITY ABBREVIATIONS

Barnston: CM6 . . . . .Barns
Bicknacre: CM3 . . . . .B'acre
Billericay: CM12-13 . . . . .Bill
Black Notley: CM7,CM77 . . . . . . .Blk N
Bocking: CM7 . . . . .Bock
Boreham: CM3 . . . . .Bor
Braintree: CM7,CM77 . . . . .Brain
Broomfield: CM1,CM3 . . . . .Broom
Chelmsford: CM1-4 . . . . .Chelm
Chignal St James: CM1 . . . . . . .Chig J
Chignal Smealy: CM1 . . . . .Chig S
Coggeshall: CO5-6 . . . . .Cogg
Cooksmill Green: CM1 . . . . .Coo G
Cressing: CM77 . . . . .Cres
Danbury: CM3 . . . . .Dan
East Hanningfield: CM3 . . . . . . .E Han
Edney Common: CM1 . . . . .E Com
Faulkbourne: CM8 . . . . .Fau
Feering: CO5 . . . . .Fee
Fryerning: CM4 . . . . .Fry
Galleywood: CM2 . . . . .Gall
Great Baddow: CM2 . . . . .Gt B
Great Dunmow: CM6 . . . . .Gt Dun
Great Notley: CM7,CM77 . . . . . .Gt Not
Great Totham: CM9 . . . . .Gt Tot
Great Waltham: CM3 . . . . .Gt W
Hatfield Peverel: CM3 . . . . .Hat P
Heybridge: CM9 . . . . .H'bri
Highwood: CM1 . . . . .High
Howe Green: CM2 . . . . .Howe G
Howe Street: CM3 . . . . .H St
Ingatestone: CM4,CM13 . . . . .Inga
Inworth: CO5 . . . . .Inw
Kelvedon: CM8,CO5 . . . . .K'dn
Langford: CM9 . . . . .L'frd
Little Baddow: CM3,CM9 . . . . . . .Lit B
Little Braxted: CM8 . . . . .L Brax
Little Dunmow: CM6 . . . . .L Dun
Little Easton: CM6 . . . . .L Eas
Little Waltham: CM1,CM3 . . . . .Lit W
Maldon: CM9 . . . . .Mal
Margaretting: CM1,CM4 . . . . . . .Marg
Mill Green: CM4 . . . . .Mill G
Mountnessing: CM4,CM13,CM15 . . . . .Mount
Mundon: CM9 . . . . .Mun
Panfield: CM7 . . . . .Pan
Rayne: CM77 . . . . .Rayne
Rivenhall: CM8 . . . . .Riven
Roxwell: CM1 . . . . .Rox
Sandon: CM2-3 . . . . .Sando
South Woodham Ferrers: CM3 . . . . .Sth F
Springfield: CM1-2 . . . . .Spr
Stebbing: CM6 . . . . .Steb
Stisted: CM77 . . . . .Stis
Stock: CM4 . . . . .Stock
Stow Maries: CM3 . . . . .Stow M
Tiptree: CO5 . . . . .Tip
Tye Green: CM7,CM77 . . . . .Tye G
Ulting: CM3 . . . . .Ult
West Hanningfield: CM2 . . . . . .W Han
Wickham Bishops: CM8 . . . . . . .W Bis
Widford: CM1-2 . . . . .Wid
Witham: CM8 . . . . .Wthm
Woodham Ferrers: CM3 . . . . .Wdhm F
Woodham Mortimer: CM9 . . . . .Wdhm M
Woodham Walter: CM3,CM9 . . . . .Wdhm W
Writtle: CM1,CM4 . . . . .Writ

A

Abbess Cl. CM1: Chelm 3J **11**
Abbey Flds. CM3: E Han 7D **20**
Abbey La. CO6: Cogg 3C **26**
Abbotsmead CM9: H'bri 2G **25**
Abbotts Pl.
CM2: Chelm 3K **27** (2D **12**)
Abell Way CM2: Spr 1H **13**
Abercorn Ho. CM3: Bor 4F **9**
Abercorn Way CM8: Wthm 4J **23**
Acacia Dr. CM6: Gt Dun 3B **22**
CM9: Mal 5F **25**
Acacia Gdns. CM8: Wthm 2K **23**
Acer Gro.
CM1: Spr 1K **27** (1D **12**)
Achilles Way CM7: Brain 2H **5**
Acorn Av. CM7: Brain 5D **4**
Acorn Cl. CM9: H'bri 2G **25**
Acres End CM1: Chelm 1J **11**
Admirals Wlk.
CM1: Chelm 2K **11**
Aetheric Rd. CM7: Brain 4E **4**
Aire Wlk. CM8: Wthm 4G **23**
Ajax Cl. CM7: Brain 2H **5**
Alamein Rd. CM1: Chelm 6E **6**
Alan Cherry Dr.
CM1: Chelm 1H **27** (1B **12**)
Alan Haslar Ho.
CM6: Gt Dun 4C **22**
Alan Rd. CM8: Wthm 5G **23**
Albany Cl. CM1: Chelm 7D **6**
Albemarle Gdns.
CM7: Brain 2J **5**
Albemarle Link CM1: Spr 4A **8**
Albert Ct. CM7: Brain 4G **5**
Albert Gdns. CO6: Cogg 2C **26**
Albert Pl. CO6: Cogg 2C **26**
Albert Rd. CM7: Brain 4G **5**
CM8: Wthm 3J **23**
Albion Ct.
CM2: Chelm 7G **27** (4B **12**)
Albra Mead CM2: Spr 1H **13**
Aldeburgh Way CM1: Spr 7J **7**
Alderbury Lea CM3: B'acre 5H **21**
Alder Dr. CM2: Chelm 7B **12**
Alder Wlk. CM8: Wthm 2K **23**
Aldridge Cl. CM2: Spr 1G **13**
Alexander Ct. CM1: Spr 5K **7**
Alexander M.
CM2: Howe G 4K **19**
Alexander Rd. CM7: Brain 3E **4**
Alexandra M. CM7: Brain 4G **5**
Alfred M.
CM2: Chelm 6H **27** (4B **12**)
Alfreg Rd. CM8: Wthm 6F **23**
Allectus Way CM8: Wthm 6F **23**
Allens Cl. CM3: Bor 3G **9**
Allen Way CM2: Spr 1H **13**
All Saints Cl. CM1: Spr 1E **12**
Alma Dr. CM1: Chelm 3K **11**
Almond Rd. CM6: Gt Dun 3A **22**
Alpha Cl. CM7: Brain 5G **5**
Aluf Cl. CM8: Wthm 6G **23**
Alverton Cl. CM77: Gt Not 2A **4**
Alyssum Cl. CM1: Spr 6B **8**
Ambridge Rd. CO6: Cogg 1A **26**
Amcotes Pl. CM2: Chelm 5C **12**
America St. CM9: Mal 5H **25**
Amoss Rd. CM2: Gt B 5F **13**
Anchorage Hill CM9: Mal 4H **25**

Anchor La. CM9: H'bri 2H 25
Anchor St.
CM2: Chelm 7G 27 (4B 12)
Anderson Av. CM1: Chelm 7E 6
Andrew Cl. CM7: Brain 2F 5
Andrews Pl.
CM1: Chelm 3K 11
Angel La. CM6: Gt Dun 4C 22
Angle Side CM7: Brain 5H 5
Anglia Ruskin University
Chelmsford Campus
..............1H 27 (1B 12)
Rivermead Campus
..............1H 27 (1B 12)
Anglia Way CM7: Brain 5H 5
Anjou Grn. CM1: Spr 5B 8
Annonay Wlk.
CM2: Chelm 5J 27
Anson Way CM7: Brain 3J 5
Anvil Way CM1: Spr 4K 7
Apple Ct. CM1: Chelm 3K 11
Appletree Wlk. CM7: Brain 6G 5
Apple Way CM2: Gt B 7D 12
Arbour La.
CM1: Spr 1K 27 (1D 12)
Arbutus Cl. CM2: Chelm 7B 12
Archers Way CM2: Gall 4C 18
Argyle Ct. CO5: K'dn 7B 26
Argyll Rd. CM2: Spr 7B 8
Armiger Way CM8: Wthm 4K 23
Armistice Av. CM1: Spr 3K 7
Armonde Cl. CM3: Bor 3F 9
Armond Rd. CM8: Wthm 4G 23
Armstrong Cl. CM3: Dan 5H 15
ARMY & NAVY FLYOVER
..............7K 27 (5C 12)
Arnhem Gro. CM7: Brain 2E 4
Arnhem Rd. CM1: Chelm 6D 6
Arnolds Farm La.
CM13: Mount 7A 24
Arnold Way CM2: Gall 3C 18
Arthur Ct. CM1: Chelm 7E 6
Arthy Cl. CM3: Hat P 1J 9
Arun Cl. CM1: Spr 7H 7
Ash Bungs. CM7: Brain 4E 4
Ashby Rd. CM8: Wthm 7J 23
Ash Cl. CM3: Hat P 1J 9
Ashdown Cl. CM77: Gt Not 7B 4
Ash Fall CM8: Wthm 1H 23
Ashfield Cl. CM6: Gt Dun 3B 22
Ashford Rd. CM1: Chelm 3J 11
Ash Gro. CM2: Chelm 6C 12
CM6: Gt Dun 5C 22
CM9: H'bri 1K 25
Ashleigh Ct. CM4: Inga 4C 24
Ashley Grn. CM3: E Han 7D 20
Ashmeads CM2: Gt B 7D 12
Ashton Pl. CM2: Spr 2G 13
Ash Tree Cl. CM1: Chelm 3K 11
Ash Tree Cres.
CM1: Chelm 3K 11
Ashurst Dr. CM1: Spr 5J 7
Aster Ct. CM1: Spr 6A 8
Atholl Rd. CM2: Spr 7A 8
Atlantic Sq. CM8: Wthm 3J 23
Attwoods Cl. CM2: Gall 3B 18
Aubrey Cl. CM1: Chelm 5G 7
Auckland Cl. CM1: Chelm 7D 6
Audley Cl. CM77: Gt Not 1A 4
Augustine Way CM3: B'acre 4H 21
Augustus M. *CM7: Brain 5E 4*
(off Pierrefitte Way)
Augustus Way CM8: Wthm 6G 23
Aurora CM1: Chelm 2F 27 (2A 12)
Austen Cl. CM7: Brain 7G 5
Avanti Stadium 5J 5
Aveley Way CM9: Mal 7G 25
Avenue, The CM1: Spr 5B 8
CM3: Bor 3C 8
CM3: Dan 6H 15
CM6: Gt Dun 4D 22
CM7: Brain 4F 5
CM8: Wthm 4J 23
Avenue Nth. CM77: Gt Not 7B 4
Avenue Rd. CM2: Gt B 6D 12
CM4: Inga 4B 24
CM8: Wthm 3J 23
Avenue W. CM77: Gt Not 7B 4
Avila Chase CM2: Gall 5B 18
Avocet Cl. CO5: K'dn 7C 26
Avocet Way CM9: H'bri 2K 25
Avon Rd. CM1: Chelm 7B 6
Avon Wlk. CM8: Wthm 3G 23
Aylesbury Dr. CM77: Gt Not 3B 4
Ayletts CM1: Broom 1G 7
Azalea Ct. CM1: Spr 6A 8

B

Back La. CM1: Spr 3J 7
CM3: E Han 7C 20
CM3: Lit W 1J 7
CM4: Fry, Mill G 2B 24
Backnang Sq. CM2: Chelm 5J 27
Back Rd. CM1: Writ 4D 10
Backwarden Nature Reserve ...2F 21
Baddow Ct. CM2: Gt B 7G 13
Baddow Hall Av. CM2: Gt B 6G 13
Baddow Hall Cres.
CM2: Gt B 6G 13
BADDOW HOSPITAL 2G 19
Baddow Pl. Av. CM2: Gt B 7G 13
Baddow Rd.
CM2: Chelm 6H 27 (4B 12)
(not continuous)
CM2: Gt B 7K 27 (5D 12)
Baden Powell Cl. CM2: Gt B ...6H 13
Badger Gro. CM7: Brain 4H 5
Badgers Cl. CM2: Gall 5B 18
Bag La. CM4: Fry, Inga 3A 24
Bailey Bri. Rd. CM7: Brain 3E 4
Bailey Ct.
CM2: Chelm 6G 27 (4B 12)
Baker Av. CM3: Hat P 2J 9
Baker M. CM9: Mal 5H 25
Baker's La. CM3: Dan 6G 15
CM77: Blk N 3B 4
Bakers La. CM2: W Han 7B 18
CM4: Inga 3C 24
Bakers M. CM4: Inga 3C 24
Baker St.
CM2: Chelm 6F 27 (4A 12)
Baker Way CM8: Wthm 7H 23
Balmoral Ct.
CM2: Chelm 4K 27 (3C 12)
CM7: Brain 3J 5
Bamboo Cres. CM7: Brain 7H 5
Bamford Ct. CM1: Chelm 4G 27
Bankart La. CM2: Spr 1F 13
Bank End CM4: Marg 6E 16
Banks Ct. CM6: Gt Dun 4C 22
Bank St. CM7: Brain 4F 5
Bantock Way CM8: Wthm 7H 23
Barbary Lodge CM2: Chelm 3A 12
Barberry Path CM6: Gt Dun 3A 22
Barbrook Way CM3: B'acre 5G 21
Barclay Cl. CM2: Gt B 6G 13
Bardell Cl. CM1: Chelm 6E 6
Barkis Cl. CM1: Chelm 5C 6
Barley Ct. CM7: Brain 6H 5
Barleyfields CM8: Wthm 5J 23
Barley La. CM6: Gt Dun 3C 22
Barley Mead CM3: Dan 7K 15
Barlow's Reach CM2: Spr 1G 13
Barnaby Rudge CM1: Chelm 5E 6
Barnardiston Way
CM8: Wthm 3H 23
Barnard Rd. CM2: Gall 4B 18
Barnards Orchard
CM77: Rayne 5A 4
Barnes Mill Rd. CM2: Spr 3F 13
Barnetson Pl. CM6: Gt Dun 4D 22
Barnfield CO5: Fee 6C 26
Barnfield Cotts. CM9: H'bri 2J 25
Barnfield M. CM1: Chelm 6F 7
Barnfield Pl. CM8: Wthm 5H 23
Barn Grn. CM1: Spr 4K 7
Barn Mead CM2: Gall 2D 18
CM7: Brain 5K 5
Barn Vw. Rd. CO6: Cogg 3C 26
Barrack Sq.
CM2: Chelm 5H 27 (3B 12)
Barrell Cl. CM9: Mal 5H 25
Barrington Cl. CM2: Gt B 7H 13
Barrington Pl. CM4: Inga 4C 24
Barrow Chase CM2: Spr 1H 13
Bartram Av. CM7: Brain 4J 5
Barwell Way CM8: Wthm 4J 23
Baskett Ct. CM1: Chelm 4G 27
Bassetts La.
CM3: Lit B, Wdhm W 1J 15
Bates Rd. CM9: Mal 3H 25
Bath Pl. Wharf CM9: Mal 4H 25
Battle Ri. CM9: H'bri 3J 25
Bawden Way CM2: Gt B 6D 12
Bawn Cl. CM7: Brain 3F 5
Baxters CM3: Dan 6J 15
Baynes Pl. CM1: Chelm 4K 11
Beach's Dr. CM1: Chelm 2H 11
Beacon Hill CM9: Mal 5F 25
Beadel Cl. CM8: Wthm 6G 23
Beadon Dr. CM7: Brain 6G 5
Beardsley Dr. CM1: Spr 5K 7
Beards Ter. CO6: Cogg 1C 26
Beatty Gdns. CM7: Brain 3J 5
Beauchamps Cl. CM1: Spr 4A 8
Beaufort Gdns. CM7: Brain 3G 5
Beaufort Rd. CM2: Spr 1G 13
Beaulieu Blvd. CM1: Spr 5A 8
Beaulieu Sq. CM1: Spr 4A 8
Beaumont Hill CM6: Gt Dun 2B 22
Beaumont Pk. CM3: Dan 7E 14
Beaumont Pl. CM6: Gt Dun 2D 22
CM7: Brain 4H 5
Beaumont Wlk. *CM1: Chelm 7C 6*
(off Chignall Rd.)
Beaumont Way CM9: Mal 7J 25
Beckers Grn. Rd. CM7: Brain 6K 5
Becketts Ct. CM1: Chelm 2F 27
Bedford Cl. CM7: Brain 3H 5
Beech Av. CM7: Brain 2F 5
Beechers Ct. CM1: Chelm 3K 11
Beeches Cl. CM1: Chelm 3J 11
Beeches Cres. CM1: Chelm 3J 11
Beeches Rd. CM1: Chelm 3J 11
CM9: H'bri 2G 25
Beech Ri. CM3: Hat P 2J 9
Beehive La. CM2: Gall, Gt B 3B 18
Beeleigh Abbey 3F 25
Beeleigh Link CM2: Spr 2F 13
Beeleigh Rd. CM9: Mal 4G 25
Beggar Hill CM4: Fry 1A 24
Begonia Cl. CM1: Spr 6A 8
Bekeswell La.
CM2: Chelm, Gall 4K 17
Bekeswell Pl. CM2: Gall 4C 18
Belgrave Cl. CM2: Gt B 6D 12
Belgrave Pl. CM2: Spr 7A 8
Bellamy Ct. CM1: Chelm 3F 27
Bellcroft CM8: Wthm 3J 23
Belle Vue CM2: Chelm 4A 12
Bellfield Cl. CM8: Wthm 3H 23
Bell Hill CM3: Dan 6E 14
Bellingham Pl. CO5: K'dn 6B 26
Bell Mead CM4: Inga 4C 24
Bellmead
CM1: Chelm 5G 27 (3B 12)
Bells Chase CM2: Gt B 7E 12
Bell St. CM2: Gt B 7F 13
Belmonde Dr. CM1: Spr 5K 7
Belmont Cl. CM1: Spr 5K 7
Belsteads Farm La.
CM3: Lit W 2K 7
Belvawney Cl. CM1: Chelm 6D 6
Belvedere Cl. CM3: Dan 6H 15
Belvedere Ct. CM2: Chelm 4K 11
CM9: Mal 7G 25
Belvedere Pl. CM9: Mal 7G 25
Belvedere Rd. CM3: Dan 6H 15
Belvoir, The CM4: Inga 4B 24
Benbridge Cl. CM9: H'bri 2H 25
Benbridge Ind. Est.
CM9: H'bri 2H 25
Benedict Dr. CM1: Chelm 3J 11
Benfield Way CM7: Brain 5H 5
Bennett Cl. CM7: Brain 7G 5
Bennett Way CM3: Hat P 1J 9
Ben Sainty Ct. *CM8: Wthm 4J 23*
(off Collingwood Rd.)
Bentalls Complex CM9: H'bri ...2J 25
Bentalls Shop. Cen.
CM9: H'bri 2J 25
Bentley Rd. CM8: Wthm 2G 23
Benton Cl. CM8: Wthm 7J 23
Benton Hall Golf Course 7J 23
Berbice La. CM6: Gt Dun 2B 22
Bergen Ct. *CM9: Mal 7G 25*
(off Midguard Way)
Berkely Dr. CM2: Spr 3F 13
Bernside CM7: Brain 5F 5
Berridge Ho. CM9: Mal 6J 25
Berwick Av. CM1: Chelm 5F 7
Betjeman Cl. CM7: Brain 7G 5
Bevington M. CM8: Wthm 4K 23
BICKNACRE 5H 21
Bicknacre Rd. CM3: Dan 7F 15
CM3: E Han 7E 20
Bigods La. CM6: Gt Dun 1C 22
Billers Chase CM1: Spr 5B 8
Bilton Rd. CM1: Chelm 4K 11
Binley Rd. CM2: Spr 3E 12
Birch Cl. CM7: Brain 5C 4
CM8: Wthm 2J 23
Birches Wlk. CM2: Gall 4A 18
Birch Rd. CM6: Gt Dun 3A 22
Birk Beck CM1: Spr 7H 7
Birkdale Ri. CM3: Hat P 1K 9
Bishop Hall La.
CM1: Chelm 1H 27 (1B 12)
Bishop Rd.
CM1: Chelm 2G 27 (2B 12)
Bishops Av. CM7: Brain 4H 5
Bishops Ct. Gdns.
CM2: Chelm 1E 12
Bittern Cl. CO5: K'dn 7C 26
Black Bread Cl. CM7: Brain 4K 5
Black Cft. Rd. CM8: Wthm 3K 23
Blacklock CM2: Spr 2G 13
Blackman Way CM8: Wthm 5J 23
Blackmore Rd. CM4: Fry 3A 24
Black Notley Lodge M.
CM7: Brain 7F 5
Blacksmith Cl. CM1: Spr 4K 7
Blackthorn Cl. CM1: Writ 4E 10
Blackthorn Rd. CM8: Wthm 2G 23
Blackwater Cl. CM1: Spr 6H 7
Blackwater La. CM8: Wthm 6K 23
Blackwater Leisure Cen. 6K 25
Blackwater Trad. Est.
CM9: Mal 3H 25
Blackwater Way CM7: Brain 3G 5
Blackwell Dr. CM7: Brain 2C 4
Bladon Cl. CM7: Bock 1E 4
Blake Dr. CM7: Brain 3J 5
Blake Rd. CM8: Wthm 1H 23
Blakes Wood Nature Reserve
..................3E 14
BLASFORD HILL 1G 7
Blenheim Cl. CM3: Dan 4H 21
CM7: Bock 1E 4
Blickling Rd. CM77: Gt Not 7C 4
Blind La. CM2: Sando 2A 20
Bliss Cl. CM8: Wthm 7H 23
Blott Ri. CM8: Wthm 6H 23
Bluebell Cl. CM8: Wthm 3G 23
Bluebell Grn. CM1: Spr 5K 7
Blue Mills Hill CM8: Wthm 7J 23
Blunts Hall Dr. CM8: Wthm 5F 23
Blunts Hall Rd. CM8: Wthm 5F 23
Blythe Way CM9: Mal 7H 25
Blyth's Mdw. CM7: Brain 4F 5
Blyth's Way CM77: Rayne 5A 4
BOCKING 2F 5
Bocking End CM7: Brain 4F 5
Bocking Pl. CM7: Brain 4F 5
Bodmin Rd. CM1: Spr 7J 7
Boleyns Av. CM7: Brain 1F 5
Boleyn Way CM3: Bor 3G 9
Bond St. CM1: Chelm ...4J 27 (3C 12)
CM2: Chelm 4J 27 (3C 12)
Bonington Chase CM1: Spr 6K 7
Boone Pl. CM8: Wthm 4J 23
Boons Cl. CM3: Bor 4F 9
Borda Cl. CM1: Chelm 7F 7
BOREHAM 4F 9
Boreham Ind. Est. CM3: Bor 2G 9
BOREHAM INTERCHANGE 5D 8
Boscawen Gdns. CM7: Brain 3J 5
Boswells Dr.
CM2: Chelm 4K 27 (3C 12)
Botany Dr. CM7: Brain 4K 5
Bouchers Mead CM1: Spr 5A 8
Boudicca M.
CM2: Chelm 7G 27 (4B 12)
Boulton Cotts. CM9: H'bri 2J 25
Bounderby Gro. CM1: Chelm 5D 6
Bourchier Av. CM7: Brain 2K 5
Bourne Ct. CM7: Brain 6K 5
Bouverie Rd.
CM2: Chelm 7H 27 (5B 12)
Bower Gdns. CM9: Mal 4G 25
Boydin Cl. CM8: Wthm 6G 23
Boyescroft CM6: Gt Dun 3C 22
Boyne Dr. CM1: Spr 6J 7
Brackenden Dr. CM1: Spr 5J 7
Bradbury Dr. CM7: Brain 4D 4
Braddy Ct. *CO5: K'dn 7B 26*
(off High St.)
Bradfords Ct. CM7: Brain 3G 5
Bradford St.
CM2: Chelm 7F 27 (4A 12)
CM7: Brain 3F 5
Bradley Cl. CM6: Gt Dun 2B 22
Bradwell Ct. CM7: Brain 7K 5
Braeburn Dr. CM9: Mal 6H 25

Braemar Av.
CM2: Chelm 7F **27** (5B **12**)
Braganza Way CM1: Spr 4A **8**
Braiding Cres. CM7: Brain 4K **5**
Brain Rd. CM8: Wthm 3G **23**
BRAINTREE 4F **5**
Braintree Bus Station 4F **5**
BRAINTREE COMMUNITY HOSPITAL
. . . . .4D **4**
Braintree District Mus. 4F **5**
Braintree Ent. Cen.
CM7: Brain 2D **4**
Braintree Foyer, The
CM7: Brain 5F 5
(off St Michael's Rd.)
Braintree Freeport Station
(Rail) **6H 5**
BRAINTREE GREEN **6A 4**
Braintree Leisure Cen. **3D 4**
Braintree Retail Pk.
CM77: Brain 6J **5**
Braintree Rd. CM6: Gt Dun 4D **22**
CM8: Wthm 2H **23**
CM77: Tye G 7K **5**
Braintree Station (Rail) **5G 5**
Braintree Swimming Cen. **7H 5**
Braintree Town FC **5J 5**
Bramble Ct. CM8: Wthm 2G **23**
Bramble Rd. CM8: Wthm 2G **23**
Brambles, The CM7: Brain 4E **4**
Bramley Cl. CM7: Brain 6G **5**
Bramley Pl. CM2: Gt B 6D **12**
Bramleys, The CO6: Cogg 1C **26**
Bramston Cl. CM2: Gt B 5F **13**
Bramston Grn. CM8: Wthm 2H **23**
Bramston Vw. CM8: Wthm 4H **23**
Bramston Wlk. CM8: Wthm 2H **23**
Bramwoods Rd. CM2: Gt B 5E **12**
Brancaster Dr. CM77: Gt Not 2B **4**
Brandon Rd. CM7: Brain 5D **4**
Brassie Wood CM3: Lit W 2K **7**
Braziers Cl. CM2: Gall 3C **18**
Breeds Rd. CM1: Chig S 1A **6**
Brendon Pl. CM1: Chelm 4J **11**
Brent Cl. CM8: Wthm 4G **23**
Brewery Flds. CM2: Gt B 1G **19**
Brian Cl. CM2: Chelm 7B **12**
Briarsford Witham Ind. Est.
CM8: Wthm 5K **23**
Briarswood CM1: Spr 5J **7**
Brick Ho. La. CM3: Bor 3F **9**
Brick Kiln Cl. CO6: Cogg 1C **26**
Brick Kiln Rd. CM2: Sando 6J **13**
Brick Kiln Way CM7: Brain 5K **5**
Bridge Ct. CM8: Wthm 5H **23**
Bridge End La. CM77: Gt Not 7C **4**
Bridge Mdw. CO5: Fee 6C **26**
Bridge St. CM1: Writ 4F **11**
CM8: Wthm 5H **23**
CO6: Cogg 3B **26**
Bridge Ter. CM9: H'bri 2H **25**
Bridon Cl. CM3: E Han 7D **20**
Bridport Rd. CM1: Spr 7J **7**
Bridport Way CM7: Brain 2K **5**
Brignall Pl. CM6: Gt Dun 4C **22**
Brimstone Ct. CM7: Brain 7E **4**
Bringey, The CM2: Gt B 7G **13**
Brise Cl. CM7: Brain 6G **5**
Bristowe Av. CM2: Gt B 7G **13**
Britten Cres. CM2: Gt B 5F **13**
CM8: Wthm 7H **23**
Broadoaks Cres. CM7: Brain 3K **5**
Broad Rd. CM7: Bock 1G **5**
CM7: Brain 2G **5**
Broad St. Grn. Rd.
CM9: Gt Tot, Mal 1K **25**
Broadway, The CM6: Gt Dun . . .1D **22**
Brock Cl. CM8: Wthm 6G **23**
Brockenhurst Way
CM3: B'acre 5H **21**
Brockley Rd.
CM2: Chelm 5K **27** (3D **12**)
Brockwell La. CO5: K'dn 7B **26**
Brograve Cl. CM2: Gall 3D **18**
Brompton Gdns. CM9: Mal 7F **25**
Bronte Cl. CM7: Brain 7G **5**
Bronte Rd. CM8: Wthm 1H **23**
Brook Cl. CM7: Brain 5C **4**
Brook End Rd. CM2: Spr 2H **13**
Brook End Rd. Nth. CM2: Spr . . .1G **13**
Brook End Rd. Sth. CM2: Spr . . .2H **13**
Brooke Sq. CM9: Mal 6H **25**
Brookhurst Cl. CM2: Chelm 2D **12**
Brooklands Wlk. CM2: Chelm . . .5A **12**
Brook La. CM2: Gall, Gt B 3D **18**
CM2: Spr 3H **13**
Brook St.
CM1: Chelm 2H **27** (2B **12**)
Brook Vw. CM2: Sando 7J **13**
Brook Wlk. CM8: Wthm 6H **23**
(not continuous)
BROOMFIELD **2G 7**
Broomfield Ct. CM1: Broom 1E **6**
BROOMFIELD HOSPITAL **1F 7**
Broomfield M. CM1: Chelm 6G **7**
Broomfield Rd.
CM1: Chelm 3F **27** (1A **12**)
Broomhall Cl. CM1: Broom 2G **7**
Broomhall Gdns. CM1: Broom . . .2G **7**
Broomhall Rd. CM1: Broom 2G **7**
Broomhills Ind. Est.
CM7: Brain 5C **4**
Browning Rd. CM7: Brain 7G **5**
CM9: Mal 7H **25**
Brownings Av. CM1: Chelm 7E **6**
Bruce Gro. CM2: Chelm 6A **12**
Bruce Rd. CM1: Writ 4F **11**
Brunel Rd. CM7: Brain 6G **5**
Brunwin Rd. CM77: Rayne 5A **4**
Bryant Link CM2: Spr 1H **13**
Bryony Cl. CM8: Wthm 2F **23**
Buchan Cl. CM7: Brain 7G **5**
Buckingham Ct. CM2: Spr 1F **13**
CM6: Gt Dun 5D **22**
Buckleys CM2: Gt B 6F **13**
Buckthorn Rd. CM6: Gt Dun 3A **22**
Buckwoods Rd. CM7: Brain 6F **5**
Buglers Ri. CM1: Writ 5F **11**
Bullen Wlk. CM2: Gall 3C **18**
Bull La. CM9: Mal 4H **25**
Bulrush Cl. CM7: Brain 6H **5**
Bundick's Hill CM1: Chelm 2K **11**
Bunsay Downs Golf Course **2K 15**
Bunting Cl. CM2: Chelm 1B **18**
Bunyan Rd. CM7: Brain 4E **4**
(not continuous)
Burdun Cl. CM8: Wthm 6F **23**
Bure Dr. CM8: Wthm 4F **23**
Burgess Fld. CM2: Spr 1F **13**
Burgess Springs
CM1: Chelm 4F **27** (3B **12**)
Burghley Cl. CM77: Gt Not 2A **4**
Burghley Way CM2: Chelm 6C **12**
Burgundy Ct. CM2: Chelm 5J **27**
Burnell Ga. CM1: Spr 5B **8**
Burnham Rd. CM1: Spr 7J **7**
Burns Cl. CM9: Mal 6H **25**
Burns Cres. CM2: Chelm 5B **12**
Burnside Cres. CM1: Chelm 5G **7**
Burnthouse La.
CM4: Inga, Mount 6A **24**
Burton Pl. CM2: Spr 1F **13**
Burwood Ct.
CM2: Chelm 7K **27** (4C **12**)
Bury La. CM3: Hat P 1H **9**
(not continuous)
Bushey Ley CM7: Brain 4K **5**
Butlers Cl. CM1: Broom 2G **7**
Buttercup Wlk. CM8: Wthm 2G **23**
Butterfield Rd. CM3: Bor 4F **9**
Buttermere CM77: Gt Not 1B **4**
Butt La. CM9: Mal 5H **25**
Buttsbury CM4: Inga 7E **24**
BUTT'S GREEN **3B 20**
Butt's Grn. Rd. CM2: Sando 2B **20**
Butts La. CM3: Dan 6G **15**
Butts Way CM2: Chelm 3J **17**
Buxton Rd. CO6: Cogg 2B **26**
Byford M. CM6: Gt Dun 4C **22**
Byng Gdns. CM7: Brain 3J **5**
Byron Cl. CM7: Brain 7G **5**
Byron Rd. CM2: Chelm 3D **12**

C

Calamint Rd. CM8: Wthm 3F **23**
Caldbeck Way CM77: Gt Not 2B **4**
Callow Ct.
CM2: Chelm 5F **27** (3A **12**)
Camberton Rd. CM7: Bock 1E **4**
Camborne Cl. CM1: Spr 1E **12**
Camellia Cl. CM1: Spr 6A **8**
Camelot Cl. CM1: Chelm 7E **6**
Cameron Cl. CM4: Inga 4C **24**
Campbell Cl. CM2: Chelm 6A **12**
Campbell Rd. CM8: Wthm 1H **23**
Campion Way CM8: Wthm 2G **23**
Camulus Cl. CM7: Brain 5G **5**
Cam Way CM8: Wthm 4F **23**
Canada Cotts. CM6: Gt Dun 4A **22**
Canberra Cl. CM1: Chelm 7D **6**
Can Bri. Way
CM2: Chelm 6J **27** (4C **12**)
Candytuft Rd. CM1: Spr 6A **8**
Canes Mill Ct. CM7: Brain 2G **5**
Canford Cl. CM2: Gt B 6E **12**
Cannon Leys CM2: Gall 3C **18**
Cannon M.
CM1: Chelm 4G **27** (3B **12**)
Canonium M. CO5: K'dn 7B **26**
Canons Cl. CM3: B'acre 5G **21**
Canside CM1: Chelm 5J **27**
Canterbury Way CM1: Chelm . . .1J **11**
Cant Way CM7: Brain 6J **5**
Canuden Rd. CM1: Chelm 4J **11**
Canvey Wlk. CM1: Spr 6K **7**
Capel Cl. CM1: Chelm 5G **7**
Capitol Square
Witham **5K 23**
Capons La. CM3: Dan 7J **15**
Card's Rd. CM2: Sando 7J **13**
Carmelite Way CM9: Mal 5G **25**
Carnation Cl. CM1: Spr 7A **8**
Carnegie Ct. CM1: Chelm 4G **27**
Carpenters Dr. CM77: Gt Not 1A **4**
Carraways CM8: Wthm 6K **23**
Carriage Dr. CM1: Spr 5K **7**
Carstone Pl. CM1: Chelm 6C **6**
Cartwright Wlk. CM2: Spr 3F **13**
Cassino Rd. CM1: Chelm 6D **6**
Castleden Way CM6: Gt Dun . . .2C **22**
Caswell M. CM2: Spr 3F **13**
Catcher Ct. CM4: Inga 5B **24**
Cathedral Wlk.
CM1: Chelm 4G **27** (2B **12**)
Catherine Cl. CM3: E Han 7D **20**
Causeway, The CM1: Writ 7B **10**
CM2: Gt B 6F **13**
CM6: Gt Dun 2C **22**
CM7: Brain 3F **5**
CM9: H'bri 3H **25**
Cavendish Gdns.
CM2: Chelm 2E **12**
CM7: Brain 2J **5**
Cawkwell Cl. CM2: Spr 1G **13**
Cecily Av. CM7: Brain 5E **4**
Cedar Av.
CM1: Chelm 2F **27** (2A **12**)
Cedar Av. W.
CM1: Chelm 2F **27** (2A **12**)
Cedar Chase CM9: H'bri 2K **25**
Cedar Cl. CM6: Gt Dun 3A **22**
Cedar Dr. CM8: Wthm 1J **23**
Cedars, The CM2: Spr 1F **13**
Centaur Way CM9: Mal 7H **25**
Centenary Way CM1: Spr 4A **8**
Central Sq. CM1: Chelm 5H **27**
Century Dr. CM77: Brain 5H **5**
Century Twr.
CM2: Chelm 5F **27** (3A **12**)
Chadwick Dr. CM7: Brain 4E **4**
Chalklands CM2: Howe G 3K **19**
Chalk's Rd. CM8: Wthm 3H **23**
Challis La. CM7: Brain 6F **5**
Chancellor Av. CM2: Spr 1H **13**
Chancellor Ct.
CM1: Chelm 1F **27** (1A **12**)
Chancery Pl. CM1: Writ 4F **11**
Chandlers Quay CM9: Mal 4H **25**
Channels Dr. CM3: Lit W 2J **7**
Channels Golf Course **1K 7**
Chantry Dr. CM4: Inga 4C **24**
Chantry Vw. CM8: Wthm 7J **23**
Chapel Cft. CM4: Inga 3C **24**
Chapel Hill CM7: Brain 5H **5**
Chapel La. CM3: Lit B 2D **14**
Chaplin Cl. CM2: Gall 4B **18**
Chaplin M. CM8: Wthm 7G **23**
Charlecote Rd. CM77: Gt Not 1B **4**
Charlotte Way CM8: Wthm 4K **23**
Charnwood Av. CM1: Chelm 4J **11**
Charters, The CM6: Gt Dun 2C **22**
Charter Way CM77: Brain 6J **5**
Chartwell Cl. CM7: Bock 1E **4**
Chase, The CM2: Gt B 7F **13**
CM3: Bor 4F **9**
CM3: E Han 6D **20**
CM77: Gt Not 3B **4**
CO5: K'dn 7B **26**
Chaseway CM8: Wthm 1H **23**
Chaseway, The CM7: Brain 5J **5**
Chatsworth Av. CM77: Gt Not 1A **4**
Chaucer Cl. CM9: Mal 7H **25**
Chaucer Cres. CM7: Brain 7G **5**
Chaucer Rd. CM2: Chelm 4D **12**
Chelmer Dr. CM6: Gt Dun 4D **22**
Chelmer Ind. Pk.
CM1: Chelm 1J **27** (1C **12**)
Chelmer La. CM9: H'bri 2H **25**
Chelmer Lea CM2: Gt B 6E **12**
Chelmer Pl.
CM2: Chelm 3K **27** (2C **12**)
Chelmer Rd.
CM2: Chelm, Spr
. . . . .7K **27** (4D **12**)
CM7: Brain 6J **5**
CM8: Wthm 4G **23**
Chelmer Ter. CM9: Mal 5J **25**
Chelmerton Av. CM2: Gt B 6E **12**
Chelmer Valley (Park & Ride) . . .**1J 7**
Chelmer Valley Rd.
CM1: Chelm, Spr
. . . . .1G **27** (1B **12**)
CHELMER VILLAGE **2G 13**
Chelmer Village Retail Pk.
CM2: Spr 3E **12**
Chelmer Village Way
CM2: Spr 7B **8**
CHELMSFORD . . . .**4H 27 (3B 12)**
Chelmsford Bus Station
. . . .**3F 27 (2A 12)**
Chelmsford Cathedral
. . . .**4H 27 (3B 12)**
Chelmsford City FC **6D 6**
Chelmsford Crematorium
CM1: Chelm 5K **11**
Chelmsford Golf Course **6K 11**
Chelmsford Hill CM1: Writ 2C **16**
Chelmsford Ho. CM6: Gt Dun . . .5D **22**
Chelmsford Mus. **5A 12**
CHELMSFORD PRIORY HOSPITAL
. . . .**1D 12**
Chelmsford Rd.
CM1: Chelm, Writ 4G **11**
CM3: E Han, Sando 5C **20**
CM6: Gt Dun, Barns 4D **22**
(not continuous)
CM9: Wdhm M 6K **15**
Chelmsford Rd. Ind. Est.
CM6: Gt Dun 5D **22**
Chelmsford Sport & Athletic Cen.
. . . .**6D 6**
Chelmsford Station
(Rail) . . . .**3G 27 (2B 12)**
Chelsea M. CM7: Brain 5F **5**
(Bernside)
CM7: Brain 6F **5**
(Buckwoods Rd.)
Chelwater CM2: Gt B 5D **12**
Chequers La. CM6: Gt Dun 4C **22**
CM9: Mal 5H **25**
(not continuous)
Chequers Rd. CM1: Writ 5D **10**
Cheriton Rd. CM7: Brain 6J **5**
Cherry Cres. CM6: Gt Dun 3A **22**
Cherry Gdn. La. CM2: Chelm . . .5A **12**
CM3: Dan 6J **15**
Cherry Gdn. Rd. CM9: Mal 5F **25**
Cherry Gdns. CM77: Brain 7D **4**
Cherry Tree Ri. CM8: Wthm 1J **23**
Cherry Trees CM4: Inga 3C **24**
Cherwell Dr. CM1: Chelm 7B **6**
Chess La. CM8: Wthm 4J **23**
Chester Pl. CM1: Chelm 7F **7**
Chestnut Av. CM3: Hat P 2J **9**
CM9: H'bri 1K **25**
CM77: Gt Not 7C **4**
Chestnut Ct. CM4: Inga 5B **24**
Chestnut Gro. CM7: Brain 5E **4**
Chestnut M. CM9: H'bri 1K **25**
Chestnut Vw. CM6: Gt Dun 3B **22**
Chestnut Wlk. CM1: Chelm 7F **7**
CM3: Lit B 4G **15**
CM8: Wthm 2K **23**
Cheviot Dr. CM1: Chelm 6C **6**
Chichester Dr.
CM1: Spr 1K **27** (1C **12**)
Chichester Way CM9: Mal 7J **25**
Chignal Rd.
CM1: Chelm, Chig S, Chig J
. . . . .2B **6**
CM1: Chig S 1A **6**
Chilford Ct. CM7: Brain 4D **4**
Chiltern Cl. CM1: Chelm 6C **6**
Chilton Cl. CM2: Gt B 6D **12**

Chinery Cl. CM1: Spr ... 1D 12
Chippingdell CM8: Wthm ... 2H 23
CHIPPING HILL ... 2G 23
Chipping Hill CM8: Wthm ... 3H 23
Chislett Row CM2: Chelm ... 5C 12
Christina Rd. CM8: Wthm ... 6F 23
Christy Av. CM1: Chelm ... 1K 11
Church Av. CM1: Broom ... 2F 7
Church Cl. CM15: Mount ... 7A 24
CHURCH END ... 2C 22
Church End CM6: Gt Dun ... 2C 22
Church End Vs. *CM6: Gt Dun ... 2D 22*
(off The Broadway)
Churchfield Rd. CO6: Cogg ... 1C 26
Church Gdns. CM6: Gt Dun ... 2C 22
Church Grn. CM1: Broom ... 3G 7
CO6: Cogg ... 2C 26
Church Hill CO5: K'dn ... 7A 26
Churchill Ri. CM1: Spr ... 5K 7
Churchill Rd. CM7: Bock ... 1E 4
Churchill Ter. CM7: Bock ... 1E 4
Church La.
CM1: Chelm ... 4H 27 (3B 12)
CM1: Spr ... 1D 12
CM1: Writ ... 4F 11
CM4: Inga, Marg ... 7C 16
CM7: Bock, Brain ... 1F 5
Church Mdws. CM7: Bock ... 1F 5
Church Rd. CM3: Bor, Lit B ... 4F 9
CM3: Hat P ... 1H 9
CM13: Inga, Mount ... 7A 24
CM15: Mount ... 7A 24
CO5: K'dn ... 7B 26
Church St.
CM1: Chelm ... 3H 27 (3B 12)
CM2: Gt B ... 7F 13
CM6: Gt Dun ... 2C 22
CM8: Wthm ... 1H 23
CM9: Mal ... 5J 25
CO5: K'dn ... 7A 26
CO6: Cogg ... 2C 26
Church Wlk. *CM9: Mal ... 4G 25*
(off High St.)
Chuzzlewit Dr. CM1: Chelm ... 5D 6
Cineworld Cinema
Braintree ... 7J 5
Circus, The CM6: Gt Dun ... 3A 22
Civic Theatre
Chelmsford ... 3F 27 (2A 12)
Clachar Cl. CM2: Spr ... 2G 13
Clairmont Cl. CM7: Brain ... 5F 5
Clapton Hall La.
CM6: Gt Dun ... 7C 22
(not continuous)
Clarence Cl. CM2: Spr ... 1G 13
Clarence M. CM2: Chelm ... 5A 12
Clare Rd. CM7: Brain ... 5D 4
Clarks Farm Rd.
CM3: Dan, Lit B ... 5H 15
Clarks Wood Dr. CM7: Brain ... 4K 5
Clark Way CM1: Broom ... 4F 7
Claudius Way CM8: Wthm ... 6G 23
Clavering Rd. CM7: Bock ... 1F 5
Clay Pits CM7: Brain ... 4K 5
Claypits Rd. CM3: Bor ... 3G 9
Clayshotts Dr. CM8: Wthm ... 6K 23
Clayton Way CM9: Mal ... 7H 25
Clematis Tye CM1: Spr ... 5K 7
Clements Cl. CM2: Spr ... 2H 13
Clevedon Cl. CM77: Gt Not ... 1B 4
Cleves Ct. CM3: Bor ... 3F 9
Clifton Ter. CM4: Inga ... 3D 24
Clinton Cl. CM3: E Han ... 7E 20
Cliveden Cl. CM1: Chelm ... 2J 11
Clobbs Yd. CM1: Broom ... 4G 7
Clockhouse Way CM7: Brain ... 5H 5
Cloisters, The CM7: Brain ... 2G 5
CO5: K'dn ... 7A 26
Close, The CM6: Gt Dun ... 5D 22
Clouded Yellow Cl. CM7: Brain ... 7E 4
Clunford Pl. CM1: Spr ... 5A 8
Clyde Cres. CM1: Chelm ... 1H 11
Clydesdale Rd. CM7: Brain ... 5E 4
Coach Ho. Way CM8: Wthm ... 4J 23
Coach La. CM9: Mal ... 4G 25
Coates Cl. CM9: H'bri ... 3J 25
Coates Lodge CM2: Spr ... 2G 13
Coates Quay
CM2: Chelm ... 5K 27 (3C 12)
Cobbs Pl. CM1: Spr ... 2K 27 (2D 12)
COGGESHALL ... 2C 26
Coggeshall Grange Barn ... 3B 26
Coggeshall Mus. & Heritage Cen.
... 2B 26
Coggeshall Rd.
CM7: Brain, Tye G ... 4F 5
CM77: Stis ... 4K 5
CO5: Cogg, K'dn ... 4A 26
CO5: Fee ... 3D 26, 4D 26
Colam La. CM3: Lit B ... 1E 14
Colchester Rd. CM2: Spr ... 7B 8
CM8: Wthm ... 4J 23
CM9: H'bri ... 2J 25
CO6: Cogg ... 2D 26
Coldhall La.
CM1: Marg, Writ ... 2C 16
CM4: Marg ... 2C 16
Coldnailhurst Av. CM7: Brain ... 3E 4
Colemans Bri. CM8: Wthm ... 3K 23
COLEMAN'S INTERCHANGE ... 2K 23
Colemans La. CM3: Dan ... 6F 15
Coleridge Ct. CM1: Chelm ... 7E 6
Coleridge Rd. CM9: Mal ... 6H 25
College Pl. *CM1: Chelm ... 1K 11*
(off Royal Well Pl.)
College Rd. CM7: Brain ... 4E 4
Colley Rd. CM2: Gt B ... 7G 13
Collingwood Cl. CM7: Brain ... 2J 5
Collingwood Rd. CM8: Wthm ... 3H 23
Collins Cl. CM7: Brain ... 5F 5
Collins La. CM8: Wthm ... 4J 23
Colne Chase CM8: Wthm ... 4G 23
Colne Ct. CM7: Brain ... 6J 5
Colne Ho. CM9: H'bri ... 2J 25
Colne Rd. CO6: Cogg ... 1C 26
(not continuous)
Colne Wlk. CM7: Brain ... 6K 5
Colville Cl. CM77: Gt Not ... 1B 4
Colvin Chase CM2: Gall ... 5B 18
Colyers Reach CM2: Spr ... 3G 13
Combined Military Services Mus.
... 4H 25
Comma Cl. CM7: Brain ... 6E 4
Common, The CM3: Dan ... 7G 15
CM3: E Han ... 6D 20
Common La. CM3: Lit B ... 3G 15
CM9: Wdhm W ... 2K 15
Compasses Row CM1: Chelm ... 1A 12
Comyns Pl. CM1: Writ ... 4F 11
Conan Doyle Cl. CM7: Brain ... 7G 5
Conduit St. *CM2: Chelm ... 3B 12*
(off Tindal St.)
Conifer Way CM6: Gt Dun ... 3B 22
Coniston Cl. CM77: Gt Not ... 2C 4
Connaught Gdns. CM7: Brain ... 3H 5
Conquerors Cl. CM3: Hat P ... 2K 9
Conrad Rd. CM8: Wthm ... 1G 23
Constable Ho. CM7: Brain ... 4E 4
Constable Vw. CM1: Spr ... 6A 8
Constance Cl. CM1: Broom ... 1F 7
CM8: Wthm ... 6K 23
Constantine Rd. CM8: Wthm ... 6G 23
Convent Hill CM7: Brain ... 2G 5
Convent La. CM7: Brain ... 2G 5
Conyer Cl. CM9: Mal ... 7G 25
Cook Pl. CM2: Spr ... 2F 13
Coombe Ri. CM1: Chelm ... 5G 7
Cooper Ct. CM9: Mal ... 5G 25
Cooper Dr. CM7: Brain ... 3D 4
Cooper Pk. CM7: Brain ... 3D 4
Coopers CM3: Bor ... 4F 9
Coopers Av. CM9: H'bri ... 2K 25
Coopers Cres. CM77: Gt Not ... 7C 4
Cooper's Row CM1: Chelm ... 7F 7
Copland Cl. CM1: Broom ... 3F 7
CM2: Gt B ... 5F 13
Copper Ct. CM7: Brain ... 6E 4
Copperfield Rd. CM1: Chelm ... 5C 6
Coppice Cl. CM6: Gt Dun ... 3C 22
Coppins Cl. CM2: Spr ... 1E 12
Coptfold Hall Dr. CM4: Marg ... 4B 16
Copt Hill CM3: Dan ... 7G 15
Copthorne Cl. CO6: Cogg ... 1C 26
Corinthian Sq.
CM2: Chelm ... 6G 27 (3B 12)
Cormorant Wlk. CM2: Chelm ... 1C 18
Cornel Cl. CM8: Wthm ... 2F 23
Cornelius Va. CM2: Spr ... 1H 13
Cornflower Dr. CM1: Spr ... 7A 8
Corn Hill
CM1: Chelm ... 4G 27 (3B 12)
Cornwall Cres. CM1: Chelm ... 5F 7
Cornwall Gdns. CM7: Brain ... 3H 5
Coronation Av. CM7: Brain ... 5F 5
Corporation Rd.
CM1: Chelm ... 1F 27 (1A 12)
Cotman Lodge CM1: Spr ... 5A 8
Cotswold Cres. CM1: Chelm ... 6C 6
Cottage Pl.
CM1: Chelm ... 3H 27 (2B 12)
Cottey Ho. CM2: Gall ... 4B 18
Coulde Dennis CM3: E Han ... 7D 20
Council Bungs. *CM7: Bock ... 1F 5*
(off Church La.)
Counting Ho. La.
CM6: Gt Dun ... 3C 22
County & Family Court
Chelmsford ... 6H 27 (4B 12)
County Pl.
CM2: Chelm ... 6G 27 (4B 12)
Court 1 CM8: Wthm ... 1H 23
Court 2 CM8: Wthm ... 1H 23
Court 3 CM8: Wthm ... 1H 23
Court 4 CM8: Wthm ... 1H 23
Court 5 CM8: Wthm ... 1G 23
Court 6 CM8: Wthm ... 1H 23
Court 7 CM8: Wthm ... 1H 23
Court 8 CM8: Wthm ... 1H 23
Court 9 CM8: Wthm ... 1H 23
Court 10 CM8: Wthm ... 1H 23
Court 11 CM8: Wthm ... 1H 23
Court 12 CM8: Wthm ... 1H 23
Court 13 CM8: Wthm ... 1H 23
Court 14 CM8: Wthm ... 1H 23
Court 15 CM8: Wthm ... 1H 23
Court 16 CM8: Wthm ... 1H 23
Court 17 CM8: Wthm ... 1H 23
Court 18 CM8: Wthm ... 1H 23
Court 19 CM8: Wthm ... 1H 23
Court 20 CM8: Wthm ... 1H 23
Courtauld Rd. CM7: Brain ... 3G 5
Courtaulds M. CM7: Brain ... 5F 5
Court Ind. Est.
CM2: Chelm ... 5K 27 (3C 12)
Courtland M. CM9: Mal ... 7G 25
Courtland Pl. CM9: Mal ... 7G 25
Courtlands CM1: Chelm ... 6F 7
Court Rd. CM1: Broom ... 1G 7
Court Vw. CM4: Inga ... 6A 24
Courtyard, The CM9: Mal ... 5G 25
Coval Av. CM1: Chelm ... 2A 12
Coval La.
CM1: Chelm ... 3F 27 (3A 12)
Coval Wells CM1: Chelm ... 3A 12
Coverdale CM8: Wthm ... 2G 23
Coverts, The CM1: Writ ... 4F 11
Cowdrie Way CM2: Spr ... 1H 13
Cowell Av. CM1: Chelm ... 7D 6
Cowlin Mead CM1: Chelm ... 4F 7
Cowpar M. CM7: Brain ... 7G 5
Cow Watering La. CM1: Writ ... 3C 10
Crabb's Hill CM3: Hat P ... 2H 9
Crabs Cft. CM7: Brain ... 4J 5
Craiston M. CM2: Gt B ... 1F 19
Craiston Way CM2: Gt B ... 1F 19
Cramphorn Theatre, The
Chelmsford ... 3F 27 (2A 12)
Cramphorn Wlk. CM1: Chelm ... 2K 11
Cranmer Ho. CM2: Wid ... 6K 11
Crayfields CM6: Gt Dun ... 3D 22
Crayford Cl. CM9: Mal ... 7F 25
Creance Ct. CM2: Chelm ... 3A 12
Creasen Butt Cl. CM9: H'bri ... 3H 25
Crescent Cl. CM6: Gt Dun ... 3B 22
Crescent Ct. CM9: H'bri ... 2G 25
Crescent Rd. CM2: Gt B ... 6G 13
CM9: H'bri ... 1G 25
Cress Cft. CM7: Brain ... 6K 5
Cressing Rd. CM7: Brain ... 4H 5
CM8: Fau, Wthm ... 1G 23
CM77: Tye G ... 7K 5
Cressy Quay
CM2: Chelm ... 5K 27 (3C 12)
Cricketers Cl. CM1: Broom ... 3H 7
Critchett Ter. *CM1: Chelm ... 2A 12*
(off Primrose Hill)
Crittall Ct. CM7: Brain ... 3D 4
Crittall Dr. CM7: Brain ... 3D 4
Crittall Rd. CM8: Wthm ... 3K 23
Crocus Way CM1: Spr ... 5K 7
Croft Cl. CM7: Brain ... 4G 5
Croft Ct. CM1: Spr ... 4K 7
CM6: Gt Dun ... 4D 22
Crofters Wlk. CM77: Brain ... 7D 4
Croft Rd. CO5: K'dn ... 7A 26
Croft Way CM8: Wthm ... 3J 23
Cromar Way CM1: Chelm ... 4K 11
Crompton St. CM1: Chelm ... 5K 11
(not continuous)
Cromwell Cen. CM8: Wthm ... 4K 23
Cromwell Cl. CM3: Bor ... 4E 8
Cromwell Hill CM9: Mal ... 4G 25
Cromwell La. CM9: Mal ... 4G 25
Cromwell Way CM8: Wthm ... 4G 23
CRONDON ... 7J 17
Cross Rd. CM8: Wthm ... 1H 23
CM9: Mal ... 6H 25
Crossways CM2: Chelm ... 6C 12
Crossways Hill CM3: Lit B ... 2J 15
Crouch Ct. CM7: Brain ... 6K 5
Crouch Dr. CM8: Wthm ... 4G 23
Crown Court
Chelmsford ... 3H 27 (2B 12)
Crown Mdw. CM7: Brain ... 3K 5
Crown Pas. CM1: Chelm ... 4H 27
Crows La. CM3: Wdhm F ... 7K 21
Croxall Ct. CM8: Wthm ... 4H 23
Crozier Ter. CM2: Spr ... 1H 13
Crummock Cl. CM77: Gt Not ... 2B 4
Crusader Way CM7: Brain ... 5K 5
Crushton Pl. CM1: Chelm ... 6E 6
Cuckoo Way CM77: Gt Not ... 2A 4
Culvert Cl. CO6: Cogg ... 3B 26
Culverts La. CM3: Bor ... 4H 9
Cumberland Av. CM9: Mal ... 6F 25
Cumberland Cl. CM7: Brain ... 3H 5
Cumberland Cres. CM1: Chelm ... 5F 7
Cunard Sq.
CM1: Chelm ... 3G 27 (2B 12)
Cunnington Rd. CM7: Brain ... 4J 5
Cuppers Cl. CM8: Wthm ... 5G 23
Curlew Cl. CM9: H'bri ... 2K 25
CO5: K'dn ... 7C 26
Currants Farm Rd. CM7: Brain ... 2E 4
Curzon Way CM2: Spr ... 3F 13
Cusak Rd. CM2: Spr ... 2F 13
Cut Hedge CM77: Gt Not ... 2B 4
Cutmore Pl. CM2: Chelm ... 5K 11
Cuton Gro. CM2: Spr ... 7C 8
Cuton Hall La. CM2: Spr ... 7B 8
Cut Throat La. CM8: Wthm ... 3J 23
(not continuous)
Cypress Ct. CM6: Gt Dun ... 3A 22
Cypress Dr. CM2: Chelm ... 7C 12
Cypress Gdns. CM7: Bock ... 1H 5
Cypress Rd. CM8: Wthm ... 2J 23
Cyril Dowsett Ct. CM9: Mal ... 5F 25

D

Daen Ingas CM3: Dan ... 6E 14
Daffodil Way CM1: Spr ... 5K 7
Dahlia Cl. CM1: Spr ... 7A 8
Dairy Rd. CM2: Spr ... 1F 13
Daisy Ct. CM1: Spr ... 6B 8
Dallwood Way CM7: Brain ... 4H 5
Dalrymple Cl. CM1: Spr ... 2D 12
Damases La. CM3: Bor ... 3K 9
Damask M. CM7: Brain ... 5G 5
Dame Elizabeth Ct.
CM1: Broom ... 1F 7
Dampier Rd. CO6: Cogg ... 1B 26
DANBURY ... 6F 15
Danbury Common Nature Reserve
... 1G 21
Danbury Country Pk. ... 6D 14
Danbury Palace Dr.
CM3: Dan ... 6D 14
Danbury Va. CM3: Dan ... 7J 15
Dane Rd. CM1: Chelm ... 3J 11
Daphne Cl. CM77: Gt Not ... 1B 4
Dapifer Dr. CM7: Brain ... 4K 5
D'Arcy Av. CM9: Mal ... 6J 25
D'Arcy Ct. CM9: Mal ... 5G 25
Darcy Ri. CM3: Lit B ... 4G 15
Darnay Ri. CM1: Chelm ... 6C 6
Darrell Cl. CM1: Chelm ... 6G 7
Dart Cl. CM8: Wthm ... 4F 23
Dartmouth Rd. CM1: Spr ... 6K 7
Darwin Cl. CM7: Brain ... 6F 5
David Wright Cl.
CM6: Gt Dun ... 5D 22
Davies Ct. CM7: Brain ... 5G 5
Dawn Cl. CM9: Mal ... 7J 25
Dawn Ho. CM2: Chelm ... 6J 27
Daws Cl. CM1: Writ ... 4D 10
Dawson Way CM8: Wthm ... 7H 23
Days Cl. CM1: Broom ... 4G 7
Deadman's La.
CM2: Gall, Gt B ... 2C 18
Deal Cl. CM7: Bock ... 1E 4
Deanery Gdns. CM7: Bock ... 1F 5
Deanery Hill CM7: Bock ... 1E 4
Dean Way CM1: Chelm ... 4J 11
Deben Cl. CM8: Wthm ... 4G 23

Deben Ct. CM7: Brain 6K 5
Deepdene CM4: Inga 4C 24
Deerhurst Chase CM3: B'acre ...5H 21
Deerleap Way CM7: Brain 3K 5
Deford Rd. CM8: Wthm 6F 23
Delamere Rd. CM1: Chelm 4J 11
Dell, The CM2: Gt B 7F 13
CM6: Gt Dun 3D 22
De-Marci Ct. CM7: Brain 4K 5
Dene Ct. CM1: Chelm 7C 6
Dengie Cl. CM8: Wthm 6H 23
Denholm Ct. CM8: Wthm 6H 23
Denmark Ho.
CM2: Chelm 7K 27 (5C 12)
Depot, The CM7: Brain 5F 5
Derwent Ct. CM1: Chelm 7D 6
Derwent Way CM1: Chelm 1H 11
CM77: Gt Not 2B 4
Desborough Path CM1: Spr 4A 8
De Vere Av. CM9: Mal 6J 25
De Vere Cl. CM3: Hat P 2K 9
Deverill Cl. CM1: Broom 2G 7
Devonshire Gdns.
CM7: Brain 3H 5
Dickens Cl. CM7: Brain 7G 5
Dickens Pl. CM1: Chelm 5C 6
Dilston CM3: Dan 7J 15
Discovery Cen., The
Great Notley 1A 4
Disney Cl. CM4: Inga 3C 24
Dixon Av. CM1: Chelm 1K 11
Docklands Av. CM4: Inga 3D 24
Dockwra La. CM3: Dan 6H 15
Doctors Pond CM6: Gt Dun 3C 22
Docwra Rd. CO5: K'dn 7B 26
Dog Kennel La.
CM4: Inga, Mill G 7A 16
Dolby Ri. CM2: Spr 3F 13
Dombey Cl. CM1: Chelm 5E 6
Domsey La. CM3: Lit W 1K 7
Donald Way CM2: Chelm 6C 12
Don Ct. CM8: Wthm 4F 23
Dorking Wlk. CM2: Gt B 6E 12
Dorothy L Sayers Cen. 4J 23
Dorothy Sayers Dr.
CM8: Wthm 1H 23
Dorset Av. CM2: Gt B 6D 12
Dorset Cl. CM2: Gt B 7E 12
Dorset Rd. CM9: Mal 7G 25
Doubleday Cnr. CO6: Cogg 2B 26
Doubleday Dr. CM9: H'bri 2G 25
Doubleday Gdns. CM7: Brain 2H 5
Douglas Cl. CM2: Gall 3D 18
Douglas Gro. CM8: Wthm 4F 23
Douglas Wlk. CM2: Chelm 5A 12
Dovecots, The CM9: Mal 5H 25
Dovedale Sports Cen. 5A 12
Dove La. CM2: Chelm 7A 12
Dover Cl. CM7: Bock 1E 4
Dowches Dr. CO5: K'dn 6B 26
Dowches Gdns. CO5: K'dn 6B 26
Downs, The CM6: Gt Dun 3C 22
CM9: Mal 4H 25
Downs Cres. CM6: Gt Dun 3B 22
Downs Footpath CM9: Mal 4H 25
Downs Rd. CM9: Mal 4H 25
Downsway CM1: Spr 6J 7
Drake Gdns. CM7: Brain 3J 5
Draymans Gro. CM77: Gt Not 7C 4
Drayton Cl. CM9: Mal 6H 25
Driberg Way CM7: Brain 6G 5
Driffield Cl. CO5: Fee 5C 26
Drive, The CM1: Chelm 6F 7
Drood Cl. CM1: Chelm 5E 6
Drovers Way CM2: Spr 5C 8
Drury La. CM7: Brain 4F 5
Dryden Cl. CM9: Mal 7H 25
Du Cane Pl. CM8: Wthm 4J 23
Dudley Cl. CM3: Bor 3F 9
Duffield Rd. CM2: Gt B 7D 12
Duggers La. CM7: Brain 6G 5
Dukes La. CM2: Spr 1F 13
Dukes Orchard CM1: Writ 5F 11
Dukes Pk. CM2: Spr 7B 8
Dukes Pk. Ind. Est. CM2: Spr 7B 8
(not continuous)
Dukes Rd. CM7: Brain 2E 4
Duke St. CM1: Chelm ...3F 27 (2A 12)
Dukes Wlk.
CM1: Chelm 3F 27 (2A 12)
Duncan Pl. CM2: Chelm 6A 12
Duncombe Cl. CM8: Wthm 7G 23
Dunlin Cl. CM9: H'bri 1K 25
Dunlin Ct. CO5: K'dn 7B 26
Dunmore Rd. CM2: Spr 2G 13
Dunmow Rd. CM6: L Eas 1B 22
Dunn Side
CM1: Chelm 2G 27 (2B 12)
Dunoon Cl. CM7: Brain 3K 5
Dunstable Dr. CM7: Brain 5K 5
Durrant Ct.
CM1: Chelm 1H 27 (1C 12)
Dyers Rd. CM9: Mal 5H 25
Dykes Chase CM9: Mal 4F 25

E

Eagle La. CM7: Brain 1F 5
Eagle Ri. CM3: Lit W 2K 7
Earlsfield Dr. CM2: Spr 2F 13
Earlsmead CM8: Wthm 3H 23
Easterford Rd. CO5: K'dn 7B 26
Eastern App. CM2: Spr 7A 8
Eastern Cres. CM1: Chelm 7E 6
EAST HANNINGFIELD 7D 20
E. Hanningfield Ind. Est.
CM3: E Han 7D 20
E. Hanningfield Rd.
CM2: Howe G, Sando 3K 19
Easton Rd. CM8: Wthm 3J 23
East St. CM7: Brain 4G 5
CO6: Cogg 2C 26
East Vw. CM1: Writ 4D 10
Eastways CM8: Wthm 3J 23
Eastwood Pk. CM2: Gt B 1G 19
Ebenezer Cl. CM8: Wthm 1G 23
Ebenezer Ter. CM2: Gt B 6F 13
Eckersley Rd.
CM1: Chelm 3J 27 (2C 12)
Eckersley Rd. Ind. Est.
CM1: Chelm 3J 27 (2C 12)
Eddy Downs CM1: Chelm 5F 7
Eden Cl. CM8: Wthm 3G 23
Eden Way CM1: Chelm 7B 6
Edinburgh Cl. CM8: Wthm 6J 23
Edinburgh Gdns. CM7: Brain 3H 5
Edison Cl. CM7: Brain 6F 5
Edmund Rd. CM8: Wthm 6G 23
EDNEY COMMON 1A 16
Edney Wood CM1: Writ 1C 16
Edward Bright Cl. CM9: Mal 5H 25
Edward Dr. CM2: Chelm 6C 12
Edwards Wlk. CM9: Mal 4G 25
Eglinton Dr. CM2: Spr 1H 13
Elderberry Gdns. CM8: Wthm ...2K 23
Elder Fld. CM77: Gt Not 3A 4
Elgar Dr. CM8: Wthm 7H 23
Elgin Av. CM1: Chelm 3A 12
Eliot Way CM9: Mal 6H 25
Elizabeth Av. CM8: Wthm 6J 23
Elizabeth Lockhart Way
CM7: Brain 2G 5
Elizabeth Way CM3: Hat P 1J 9
CM9: H'bri 2H 25
Ellen Way CM77: Gt Not 1B 4
Elliot Dr. CM7: Brain 4C 4
Elliot Pl. CM7: Brain 4J 5
Elm Av. CM9: H'bri 2J 25
Elm Bungs. CM7: Brain 3D 4
Elm Cl. CM1: Broom 3F 7
CM2: Gt B 7E 12
Elm Grn. La. CM3: Dan 5E 14
Elm Ri. CM8: Wthm 1H 23
Elm Rd. CM2: Chelm 5A 12
CM6: Gt Dun 2A 22
Elmscroft CM6: Gt Dun 4D 22
Elms Dr. CM1: Chelm ...1F 27 (1A 12)
Elm Way CM3: Bor 3F 9
Elsham Dr. CM77: Gt Not 2A 4
Elston Ct. CM4: Inga 3C 24
Embassy Ct. CM9: Mal 5H 25
Emberson Ct. CM2: Spr 1F 13
Emberson Cft. CM1: Chelm 4F 7
Emblems CM6: Gt Dun 2B 22
Emneth Acre CM9: Mal 6F 25
Emperor Cl. CM9: H'bri 2H 25
Empire Wlk. CM2: Chelm 5J 27
Ennerdale Av. CM77: Gt Not 2B 4
Enterprise Ct. CM7: Brain 5H 5
CM8: Wthm 3J 23
Epping Cl. CM1: Chelm 4J 11
Epping Way CM8: Wthm 5G 23
Erick Av. CM1: Chelm 5G 7
Eridge Cl. CM1: Spr 5J 7
Essex Av. CM1: Chelm 5F 7
Essex County Cricket Ground
....5G 27 (3B 12)
Essex Outdoors
Danbury 6E 14
Essex Regiment Mus. 5A 12
Essex Regiment Way
CM1: Spr 1J 7
CM3: Lit W 1J 7
Essex Rd. CM7: Brain 3H 5
CM9: Mal 6G 25
Estella Mead CM1: Chelm 5D 6
Europa Pk. CM8: Wthm 3J 23
Evelyn Pl. CM1: Chelm 5K 11
Everest Way CM9: H'bri 2J 25
Everitt Ct. CM8: Wthm 7G 23
Eves Cnr. CM3: Dan 6G 15
Eves Cres. CM1: Chelm 7F 7
Exchange Way
CM1: Chelm 4H 27 (3B 12)
Exeter Cl. CM7: Brain 2H 5
Exeter Rd. CM1: Spr 7K 7
Exley Cl. CM4: Inga 3C 24
Exmoor Cl. CM1: Chelm 4H 11

F

Faber Rd. CM8: Wthm 6G 23
Fabians Cl. CO6: Cogg 1C 26
Faggot Yd. CM7: Brain 2F 5
Fairfax Mead CM2: Spr 3F 13
Fairfield CM4: Inga 3D 24
Fairfield Chase CM9: Mal 5G 25
Fairfield Ho. CM9: Mal 5G 25
Fairfield Rd.
CM1: Chelm 3F 27 (2A 12)
CM7: Brain 5F 5
Fairleads CM3: Dan 5H 15
Fair Vw. CM6: Gt Dun 4C 22
Fairway CM2: Gt B 6D 12
Fairway Dr. CM3: Lit W 2K 7
Fairy Hall La. CM77: Rayne 7A 4
Falcon Bowling & Social Club ...2J 7
Falcon Flds. CM9: Mal 7G 25
Falcon M. CM9: Mal 7G 25
Falcons Mead CM2: Chelm 4A 12
Falcon Way CM2: Chelm 7A 12
Fal Dr. CM8: Wthm 4G 23
Falkland Cl. CM3: Bor 4F 9
Falkland Ct. CM7: Brain 3H 5
Falmouth Rd. CM1: Spr 7K 7
Fambridge Cl. CM9: Mal 6H 25
Fambridge Rd. CM9: Mal 5G 25
(not continuous)
Faraday Cl. CM7: Brain 6F 5
FARLEIGH DAY HOSPICE (MALDON)
....2J 25
FARLEIGH HOSPICE (CHELMSFORD)
....1F 7
Farriers Way CM77: Gt Not 1A 4
Farrow Rd. CM1: Wid 6J 11
Farthing Cl. CM7: Brain 3K 5
Faulkbourne Rd.
CM8: Fau, Wthm 2F 23
Fawkner Cl. CM2: Spr 3F 13
Feather Cl. CM7: Brain 5K 5
Feering & Kelvedon
Local History Mus. 7A 26
Feering Hill CO5: Fee 6C 26
Feering Rd. CO6: Cogg 2D 26
Felbrigg Cl. CM77: Gt Not 1A 4
Fell Christy CM1: Chelm 7G 7
Fenton Ct. CM1: Chelm 3F 27
Ferndown Way CM3: Hat P 1K 9
Fernie Rd. CM7: Brain 5D 4
Fifth Av. CM1: Chelm 6F 7
Fillioll Cl. CM3: E Han 7D 20
Finch Dr. CM7: Brain 2D 4
Finchley Av. CM2: Chelm 5A 12
Firecrest Rd. CM2: Chelm 1C 18
Firs Dr. CM1: Writ 4F 11
First Av. CM1: Chelm 7F 7
Fir Tree La. CM3: Lit B 4G 15
Fir Tree Ri. CM2: Chelm 7A 12
Fir Tree Wlk. CM9: H'bri 2K 25
Fisher Way CM7: Brain 3J 5
Fitch's Cres. CM9: Mal 6J 25
Fitch's M. CM9: Mal 6J 25
Fitzwalter La. CM3: Dan 7F 15
Fitzwalter Pl. CM1: Chelm 2J 11
CM6: Gt Dun 4C 22
Fitzwalter Rd. CM3: Bor 4G 9
Five Acres CM3: Dan 3H 21
Flanders Cl. CM7: Brain 2E 4
Fleetwood Sq. CM1: Spr 4A 8
Fleming Cl. CM7: Brain 6F 5
Flintwich Mnr. CM1: Chelm 5D 6
Flitch Fitness Cen. 5C 22
Flitch Ind. Est. CM6: Gt Dun 5C 22
Flitch La. CM6: Gt Dun 5D 22
Flora Rd. CM8: Wthm 2F 23
Fordson Rd. CM2: Spr 6C 8
Fore Fld. CM7: Brain 4K 5
Forefield Grn. CM1: Spr 5A 8
Foremans CM1: Chelm 2J 11
Forest Dr. CM1: Chelm 3J 11
Forest Rd. CM8: Wthm 1J 23
Forsyth Dr. CM7: Brain 7G 5
Forsythia Cl. CM1: Spr 5K 7
Fortinbras Way CM2: Chelm 6B 12
Foster Ct. CM8: Wthm 4J 23
Fosters Cl. CM1: Writ 4D 10
Fourth Av. CM1: Chelm 7F 7
Fowler Ct. CM2: Chelm 2A 18
Fox Burrows La. CM1: Writ 3F 11
Fox Cres. CM1: Chelm 1K 11
Foxglove Cl. CM8: Wthm 3F 23
Foxglove Way CM1: Spr 6A 8
Foxholes Rd. CM2: Gt B 7F 13
Framlingham Way
CM77: Gt Not 2B 4
Frances Grn. CM1: Spr 5B 8
Francis M. CM9: Mal 7J 25
Francis Rd. CM7: Brain 5D 4
Fraser Cl. CM2: Chelm 5C 12
Frating Ct. CM7: Brain 6K 5
Freebournes Ct. CM8: Wthm ...4J 23
Freebournes Rd. CM8: Wthm ...3K 23
Freebournes Rd. Ind. Est.
CM8: Wthm 3K 23
Freeman Ct. CM1: Chelm 4G 27
Freeport Braintree
CM77: Brain 6H 5
Freeport Office Village
CM77: Brain 6H 5
French's Wlk. CM2: Chelm 5J 27
Freshwater Cres. CM9: H'bri 3J 25
Fresian Cl. CM7: Brain 5C 4
Friars Cl. CM2: Gt B 7G 13
Friars La. CM7: Brain 3F 5
CM9: Mal 5G 25
Friars Wlk.
CM2: Chelm 6H 27 (3B 12)
Friary Flds. CM9: Mal 5H 25
Frobisher Cl. CM9: Mal 7H 25
Frobisher Way CM7: Brain 3J 5
FRYERNING 2B 24
Fryerning La. CM4: Fry, Inga ...2B 24
Fulcher Av. CM2: Spr 2F 13
Fullbridge CM9: Mal 4H 25
Fuller's Cl. CO5: K'dn 7A 26
Fullers Ga. CO5: K'dn 7A 26
Furlongs, The CM4: Inga 3B 24
Further Mdw. CM1: Writ 5E 10
FURZE HILL INTERCHANGE ...6D 16

G

Gablefields CM2: Sando 7J 13
Gadwall Reach CO5: K'dn 7C 26
Gaiger Cl. CM1: Spr 5J 7
Gainsborough Cres.
CM2: Chelm 2E 12
Galleydene Av. CM2: Gall 3C 18
GALLEYEND 3D 18
GALLEY RDBT. 6K 5
Galleys Cnr. CM77: Tye G 7K 5
GALLEYWOOD 3B 18
Galleywood Rd. CM2: Chelm ...7A 12
CM2: Gt B 2D 18
GALLEYWOOD / STOCK INTERCHANGE
....6B 18
Galliford Rd. CM9: H'bri 3H 25
Galliford Rd. Ind. Est.
CM9: H'bri 2H 25
Galsworthy Cl. CM7: Brain 7G 5
Gardeners CM2: Gt B 1D 18
Gardeners Row CO6: Cogg 2C 26
Garden Fld. CM3: Hat P 1H 9
Garrettlands CM2: Sando 7B 14
Gatehouse M. CM4: Inga 4C 24
Gatehouse Vs. CM6: Gt Dun 5D 22
Gatekeeper Cl. CM7: Brain 6F 5
Gate St. CM9: Mal 4G 25
Gate St. M. CM9: Mal 4G 25
Gauden Rd. CM7: Bock 1F 5
GAY BOWERS 1J 21
Gay Bowers La. CM3: Dan 6H 15
Gay Bowers Rd. CM3: Dan 2G 21

Gay Bowers Way CM8: Wthm . . .7J **23**
Generals La. CM3: Bor 2C **8**
Geoffrey Blackwell Cl.
CO6: Cogg 2B **26**
George Ct.
CM2: Chelm 6G **27** (4B **12**)
George Free Path *CM9: H'bri . . .2K 25*
(off Lawling Av.)
George Rd. CM7: Brain 4D **4**
George St.
CM2: Chelm 7G **27** (4B **12**)
George Yd. CM7: Brain 4F **5**
George Yd. Shop. Cen.
CM7: Brain 4F **5**
Gepp Pl. CM2: Spr 1H **13**
Gerard Gdns. CM2: Gt B 5D **12**
Gernon Cl. CM1: Broom 1G **7**
Gershwin Blvd. CM8: Wthm 7H **23**
Gibbons Ct. CM6: Gt Dun 3C **22**
Gibson Va. CM1: Broom 4G **7**
Giffins Cl. CM7: Brain 6E **4**
Gilbert Way CM7: Brain 2J **5**
Gilchrist Way CM7: Brain 3E **4**
Gilda Ter. CM77: Brain 5B **4**
Gill Cl. CM9: H'bri 1G **25**
Gilmore Pl. CM2: Gt B 6H **13**
Gilmore Way CM2: Gt B 6H **13**
Gilpin Way CM77: Gt Not 1B **4**
Gilson Cl. CM2: Spr 3F **13**
Gimson Cl. CM8: Wthm 4H **23**
Gladstone Ct.
CM2: Chelm 7H **27** (4B **12**)
Glebe Av. CM7: Bock 1F **5**
Glebe Cres. CM1: Broom 3G **7**
CM8: Wthm 2G **23**
Glebefield Rd. CM3: Hat P 1K **9**
Glebe Rd.
CM1: Chelm 2F **27** (2B **12**)
CM9: H'bri 2K **25**
CO5: K'dn 7A **26**
Glebe Vw. CM2: Gall 3B **18**
Gleneagles Way CM3: Hat P 1K **9**
Glenway Cl. CM9: Mal 7J **25**
Gloucester Av. CM2: Chelm 6A **12**
CM9: Mal 6G **25**
Gloucester Cres. CM1: Chelm 7F **7**
Gloucester Gdns. CM7: Brain 3H **5**
Glovershotts CM1: Broom 2G **7**
Goat Hall La. CM2: Chelm 4K **17**
Goda Cl. CM8: Wthm 6F **23**
Goddard Way CM2: Spr 3F **13**
Godfrey's M.
CM2: Chelm 7G **27** (4B **12**)
Godfrey Way CM6: Gt Dun 2B **22**
Godlings Way CM7: Brain 5E **4**
Godric Pl. CM7: Brain 4E **4**
Godric Rd. CM8: Wthm 6G **23**
Godwit Ct. CO5: K'dn 7C **26**
Goings Wharf Ind. Est.
CM9: H'bri 2J **25**
Goldenacres CM1: Spr 4A **8**
Goldhanger Ct. CM7: Brain 7K **5**
Goldhanger Rd.
CM9: H'bri, Mal 2K **25**
Goldingham Dr. CM7: Brain 7G **5**
Golding Thoroughfare
CM2: Spr 1F **13**
Goldlay Av.
CM2: Chelm 7K **27** (5C **12**)
Goldlay Gdns.
CM2: Chelm 7J **27** (4C **12**)
Goldlay Rd.
CM2: Chelm 7J **27** (4C **12**)
Goldsmith Ct. CM1: Chelm 4F **27**
Goodier Rd. CM1: Chelm 2K **11**
Goodwin Cl. CM2: Gt B 5D **12**
Gordon Carlton Gdns.
CM1: Spr 3K **7**
Gordon Rd. CM2: Chelm 7A **12**
Gore, The CM77: Rayne 5A **4**
Gore La. CM77: Rayne 5A **4**
GORE PIT **5D** 26
Gore Rd. CM77: Rayne 5A **4**
Gore Ter. CM77: Rayne 5A **4**
Goshawk Dr. CM2: Chelm 1B **18**
Goulton Rd. CM1: Broom 3F **7**
Gowers Av. CM2: Gt B 7E **12**
Grace Bartlett Gdns.
CM2: Chelm 6K **11**
Graces Cl. CM8: Wthm 7J **23**
Graces La. CM3: Lit B 4D **14**
Grace's Wlk.
CM3: Lit B, Sando 3A **14**
Grafton Pl. CM2: Spr 1G **13**
Graham Brown Wlk.
CM8: Wthm 7G **23**
Grampian Gro.
CM1: Chelm 6C **6**
Granary Ct. CM6: Gt Dun 4C **22**
Grange Ct. CM2: Wid 6K **11**
Grange Hill CO6: Cogg 3B **26**
Granger Av. CM9: Mal 6G **25**
Granger Row CM1: Chelm 6E **6**
Grantham Av. CM77: Gt Not 1A **4**
(not continuous)
Grasmere Cl. CM77: Gt Not 2B **4**
Gravel, The CO6: Cogg 2B **26**
Gravelly La. CM1: Rox 2A **10**
Grayling Cl. CM7: Brain 6E **4**
Grays Brewery Yd.
CM2: Chelm 5J **27** (3C **12**)
GREAT BADDOW **6F** 13
Great Cob CM1: Spr 7K **7**
GREAT DUNMOW **4C** 22
Great Dunmow Leisure Cen. . . .**2A** 22
Great Dunmow Maltings &
Great Dunmow Mus. **3C** 22
Gt. Gibcracks Chase
CM2: Sando 4C **20**
Great Godfreys CM1: Writ 4D **10**
GREAT NOTLEY **1B** 4
Gt. Notley Av. CM77: Gt Not 3B **4**
Great Notley Country Pk. **7A** 4
GREAT OXNEY GREEN **4C** 10
Great Sq. CM7: Brain 4F **5**
Green, The CM1: Chelm 1K **11**
CM1: Writ 4F **11**
CM3: Hat P 2K **9**
Green Acres CO6: Cogg 3B **26**
Greenbury Way
CM1: Wid, Writ 5D **10**
Green Cl. CM1: Spr 1D **12**
CM1: Writ 4F **11**
CM3: Hat P 2K **9**
Greene Vw. CM7: Brain 7H **5**
Greenfield CM8: Wthm 5J **23**
Greenland Gdns. CM2: Gt B 7F **13**
Green La. CM6: Gt Dun 3B **22**
Green Mdws. CM3: Dan 7J **15**
Greenway Gdns. CM77: Brain 1C **4**
Greenways CM1: Chelm 6G **7**
CM9: Mal 5G **25**
CO5: Fee 6C **26**
Greenways, The CO6: Cogg 1C **26**
Greenways Chase CM9: Mal 5F **25**
Greenwell Rd. CM8: Wthm 7H **23**
Greenwood Cl. CM2: Spr 3F **13**
Grenville Rd. CM7: Brain 5E **4**
Gresley Dr. CM7: Brain 5G **5**
Grey Ladys CM2: Gall 4B **18**
Groom Side CM7: Brain 5G **5**
Grosvenor Cl. CM2: Gt B 6D **12**
Grove, The CM3: B'acre 5H **21**
CM8: Wthm 4J **23**
Grove Cen., The CM8: Wthm . . .5J **23**
Grove Ct. CM6: Gt Dun 5D **22**
Grove Rd.
CM2: Chelm 7H **27** (4B **12**)
Guernsey Ct. CM9: Mal 5G **25**
Guernsey Way CM7: Brain 5C **4**
Guilder Rose CM6: Gt Dun 3A **22**
Guinea Cl. CM7: Brain 3K **5**
Guithavon Ri. CM8: Wthm 4H **23**
Guithavon Rd. CM8: Wthm 5H **23**
Guithavon St. CM8: Wthm 4H **23**
Guithavon Valley
CM8: Wthm 4H **23**
Gulls Cft. CM7: Brain 4J **5**
Gunson Ga. CM2: Chelm 6D **12**
Gurton Rd. CO6: Cogg 1C **26**
Gutters La.
CM1: Broom, Chelm 5G **7**
Guys Farm CM1: Writ 4F **11**
Gwyn Cl. CM3: Bor 3F **9**

H

Hadfelda Sq. CM3: Hat P 1J **9**
Hadrians Cl. CM8: Wthm 6G **23**
Hadrians Way CM9: H'bri 3H **25**
Haig Ct. CM2: Chelm 4A **12**
Hainault Gro. CM1: Chelm 4J **11**
Halcyon Cl. CM8: Wthm 6G **23**
Halfacres CM8: Wthm 7J **23**
Hall Bri. Ri. CM9: H'bri 3K **25**
Hall Cl. CM2: Gt B 7G **13**
Hall Farm Cl. CO5: Fee 5D **26**
Hall La. CM2: Sando 7J **13**
(not continuous)
CM4: Inga 5C **24**
Hall Ri. CM8: Wthm 6H **23**
Hall Rd. CM9: H'bri, Mal 3J **25**
Hall St. CM2: Chelm . . .6H **27** (4B **12**)
Halston Pl. CM9: Mal 7G **25**
Hamble Cl. CM8: Wthm 4G **23**
Hamilton Ct. CM1: Chelm 6C **6**
Hamlet Rd.
CM2: Chelm 7G **27** (4B **12**)
Hammonds Rd. CM2: Sando 4K **13**
CM3: Lit B, Sando 4K **13**
Hampton Rd. CM2: Gt B 7E **12**
Hanbury Rd. CM1: Wid 5J **11**
Hance La. CM77: Rayne 5A **4**
HANDLEY GREEN **6B** 16
Hanlee Brook CM2: Gt B 1F **19**
Hanover Ct. CM8: Wthm 5J **23**
Harberd Tye CM2: Gt B 6D **12**
Harding's La. CM4: Inga 1A **24**
Hardwick Cl. CM77: Gt Not 1A **4**
Hardy Cl. CM1: Chelm 3A **12**
CM7: Brain 7G **5**
Hardy Wlk. CM8: Wthm 7G **23**
Harebell Dr. CM8: Wthm 3G **23**
Hare Bri. Cres. CM4: Inga 5A **24**
Harewood Rd. CM1: Chelm 4J **11**
Harkilees Way CM7: Brain 2F **5**
Harlings Gro.
CM1: Chelm 3J **27** (2B **12**)
Harmans Yd. CM6: Gt Dun 4C **22**
Harness Cl. CM1: Spr 5K **7**
Harnham Dr. CM77: Gt Not 1B **4**
Harold Ri. CM9: H'bri 2G **25**
Harold Rd. CM7: Brain 4E **4**
Harrington Mead CM2: Spr 2H **13**
Harris Grn. CM6: Gt Dun 5D **22**
Harrison Ct. CM1: Chelm 2K **11**
Harrison Dr. CM7: Brain 6G **5**
Harrow Way CM2: Gt B 7G **13**
Hartley Cl. CM2: Spr 1G **13**
Hartley Ho. CM7: Brain 5J **5**
Hart St. CM2: Chelm 4A **12**
Harvest Ct. CO5: Fee 5D **26**
Harvest Way CM9: H'bri 2G **25**
Harwell Cl. CM7: Brain 3K **5**
Haselfoot Rd. CM3: Bor 4G **9**
Haskell M. CM7: Brain 7G **5**
Hasler Pl. CM6: Gt Dun 4C **22**
Haslers Ct. CM4: Inga 3D **24**
Haslers La. CM6: Gt Dun 4C **22**
Hatches M. CM7: Brain 3K **5**
Hatfield Gro. CM1: Chelm 4H **11**
(not continuous)
HATFIELD PEVEREL **1H** 9
HATFIELD PEVEREL
INTERCHANGE NORTH **1J** 9
HATFIELD PEVEREL
INTERCHANGE SOUTH **1H** 9
Hatfield Peverel Station
(Rail) **1H** 9
Hatfield Rd. CM3: Hat P, Lit B . . .4K **9**
CM8: Wthm 7F **23**
Haven Ct. CM3: Hat P 1H **9**
Havencourt
CM1: Chelm 3H **27** (2B **12**)
Havengore CM1: Spr 7K **7**
Havisham Way CM1: Chelm 5D **6**
Hawfinch Wlk. CM2: Chelm 1B **18**
Hawkes Rd. CM8: Wthm 7G **23**
CO6: Cogg 1B **26**
Hawkhurst Cl. CM1: Chelm 3J **11**
Hawkins Way CM7: Brain 3J **5**
Hawks Cl. CM3: Dan 1J **21**
Hawthorn Cl. CM2: Chelm 7C **12**
Hawthorn Ri. CM8: Wthm 1J **23**
Hawthorn Rd. CM3: Hat P 1J **9**
Hawthorns, The CM3: Dan 6J **15**
Hawthorn Way CM6: Gt Dun 2B **22**
Hayes Cl.
CM2: Chelm 6G **27** (4B **12**)
Hay Grn. CM3: Dan 5H **15**
Haygreen Rd. CM8: Wthm 7G **23**
Hay La. Nth. CM7: Brain 4J **5**
Hay La. Sth. CM7: Brain 4J **5**
Haymeads Ct. CM9: H'bri 2H **25**
Haytor Cl. CM7: Brain 5J **5**
Hazel Cl. CM6: Gt Dun 3B **22**
CM8: Wthm 2J **23**
Hazel Gro. CM7: Brain 6E **4**
Hazelwood Ct. CM9: H'bri 1J **25**
Hearsall Av. CM1: Chelm 5G **7**
Heath Dr. CM2: Chelm 7B **12**
Heather Ct. CM1: Spr 6A **8**
Heathfield Rd. CM1: Chelm 4G **7**
Hedgerows Bus. Pk. CM2: Spr . . .6B **8**
Heights, The CM3: Dan 6E **14**
Helford Ct. CM8: Wthm 4F **23**
Helston Rd. CM1: Spr 6K **7**
Hemingway Rd. CM8: Wthm . . .1H **23**
Hemlock Cl. CM8: Wthm 2J **23**
Hemmings Ct. CM9: Mal 7F **25**
Henderson Way CM8: Wthm . . .6K **23**
Henniker Ga. CM2: Spr 1G **13**
Henry Rd.
CM1: Chelm 1G **27** (1B **12**)
Hereford Ct. CM2: Gt B 1G **19**
Hereford Dr. CM7: Brain 2K **5**
Hering Dr. CM9: H'bri 3K **25**
Heron Rd. CO5: K'dn 7C **26**
Heron Way CM9: H'bri 2K **25**
Herringham Grn. CM2: Spr 1G **13**
Hewitt Wlk. CM8: Wthm 4J **23**
HEYBRIDGE
CM4 . . . .**6A** 24
CM9 . . . .**2J** 25
Heybridge App. CM9: H'bri 1G **25**
Heybridge Hall Gdns.
CM9: H'bri 3J **25**
Heybridge Ho. Ind. Est.
CM9: Mal 3J **25**
Heybridge Rd. CM4: Inga 6A **24**
Heybridge St. CM9: H'bri 2J **25**
Heycroft Way CM2: Gt B 1F **19**
Heythrop, The CM2: Chelm 1D **12**
CM4: Inga 4B **24**
Heywood Ct. CM9: H'bri 1J **25**
Heywood La. CM6: Gt Dun 5C **22**
Heywood Way CM9: H'bri 1J **25**
Hidcote Way CM77: Gt Not 1A **4**
High Bri. Rd.
CM2: Chelm 6J **27** (4C **12**)
High Chelmer
CM1: Chelm 5G **27** (3B **12**)
High Chelmer Shop. Cen.
CM1: Chelm 4G **27**
Highclere Rd. CM77: Gt Not 2A **4**
High Elms CM7: Brain 7F **5**
Highfield Cl. CM3: Dan 7F **15**
CM7: Brain 1G **5**
Highfield Rd. CM1: Chelm 1J **11**
High Flds. CM6: Gt Dun 4B **22**
CM8: Wthm 4G **23**
Highfields Mead CM3: E Han . . .6D **20**
Highfields Rd. CM8: Wthm 3G **23**
Highfield Stile Rd. CM7: Brain . . .1G **5**
Highlands Dr. CM9: Mal 5F **25**
High Mdw. CM6: Gt Dun 4B **22**
High Pasture CM3: Lit B 2F **15**
High Stile CM6: Gt Dun 4B **22**
High St. CM1: Chelm . . .4H **27** (3B **12**)
CM2: Gt B 6F **13**
CM4: Inga 5B **24**
CM6: Gt Dun 4C **22**
CM7: Brain 5E **4**
CM9: Mal 4G **25**
CO5: K'dn 7A **26**
Highwood Rd.
CM1: E Com, High 1A **16**
CM1: Writ 6C **10**
Hillary Cl. CM1: Spr . . .1K **27** (1D **12**)
CM9: H'bri 2J **25**
Hill Cres. CM2: Chelm 3D **12**
Hillfield CO5: Fee 5C **26**
Hill Ho. Pk. CM9: Mal 4G **25**
Hill Rd. CM2: Chelm 3D **12**
CO6: Cogg 2D **26**
Hill Rd. Sth. CM2: Chelm 4D **12**
Hills Cl. CM7: Brain 3F **5**
Hillside CM9: Mal 4H **25**
Hillside Gdns. CM7: Brain 6F **5**
Hillside Gro. CM2: Chelm 7A **12**
Hillside Ho. CM7: Brain 6F **5**
Hillside M. CM2: Chelm 6A **12**
Hillside Ter. CM7: Brain 6F **5**
Hillview CM3: B'acre 5H **21**
Hill Vw. Rd.
CM1: Spr 1K **27** (1C **12**)
Hillway, The CM4: Inga 7A **24**
CM15: Mount 7A **24**
Hitcham M. CM7: Brain 7H **5**
Hitcham Rd. CO6: Cogg 1B **26**
Hitchcock's Meadows Nature Reserve
. . . .**7H** 15
HMP & YOI Chelmsford
CM2: Chelm 2D **12**
Hobart Cl. CM1: Chelm 7D **6**

Hoblongs Ind. Est. CM6: Gt Dun 6D 22
Hodge Ct. CM1: Chelm 2F 27 (2A 12)
Hodges Holt *CM8: Wthm 7J 23 (off Maldon Rd.)*
Hoe St. CM1: Rox 1A 10
Hoffmanns Way CM1: Chelm 1H 27 (1B 12)
Hogarth Ct. *CM1: Spr 6K 7 (off Rembrandt Gro.)*
Holden Cl. CM7: Brain 5G 5
Hollis Lock CM2: Spr 2G 13
Holloway Rd. CM9: H'bri 1G 25
Hollow La. CM1: Broom, Chelm, Chig S 5C 6
Hollybank CM8: Wthm 5H 23
Holly Brook CM7: Brain 3G 5
Holly Cl. CM6: Gt Dun 3B 22
Hollycroft CM2: Gt B 7H 13
Holly Wlk. CM8: Wthm 1K 23
Holly Way CM2: Chelm 6D 12
Hollywood Cl. CM2: Gt B 7E 12
Holmans CM3: Bor 4F 9
Holm Dr. CM6: Gt Dun 3A 22
Holst Av. CM8: Wthm 7G 23
Holybread La. CM3: Lit B 1E 14
Home Bri. Ct. CM8: Wthm 6H 23
Homefield Cl. CM1: Chelm 7C 6
Homefield Rd. CM8: Wthm 2J 23
Home Mead CM1: Writ 4E 10
CM2: Gall 4C 18
Homestead CM1: Broom 5G 7
Honey Cl. CM2: Gt B 7C 12
Honeypots CM2: Gt B 7C 12
Honeysuckle Path CM1: Spr 6A 8
Honeysuckle Way CM8: Wthm 2F 23
Honeywood Av. CO6: Cogg 1C 26
Honor Link CM1: Spr 5B 8
Honywood Gdns. CM2: Chelm 7K 27 (5C 12)
Hood Gdns. CM7: Brain 3J 5
Hope Cl. CM15: Mount 7A 24
Hopes La. CM4: Marg 6G 17
Hopkins Mead CM2: Spr 3F 13
Hopkirk Cl. CM3: Dan 5H 15
Hoppet, The CM4: Inga 3D 24
Hopping Jacks La. CM3: Dan 6H 15
Hoppit Mead CM7: Brain 6F 5
Hopwood Vw. CM2: Gt B 7D 12
Hornbeam Cl. CM2: Chelm 7A 12
Hornbeam Wlk. CM8: Wthm 2J 23
HORNE ROW 1F 21
Horne Row CM3: Dan 7F 15
Horner Pl. CM8: Wthm 4J 23
Horn La. CO6: Cogg 2C 26
Horse & Groom La. CM2: Chelm, Gall 4A 18
Horton Cl. CM9: Mal 6H 25
Hospital App. CM1: Broom 1F 7
Houblon Dr. CM2: Gall 4C 18
Howard Cl. CM7: Brain 4H 5
Howard Dr. CM2: Spr 3G 13
Howards Cl. CM3: Bor 4F 9
Howbridge Hall Rd. CM8: Wthm 7H 23 (Maldon Rd.)
CM8: Wthm 7H 23 (Pondholton Dr.)
Howbridge Rd. CM8: Wthm 6H 23
HOWE GREEN 4K 19
HOWE GREEN INTERCHANGE 2H 19
Hoynors CM3: Dan 6J 15
Hub, The CM77: Gt Not 7A 4
Hull's La. CM2: Sando 7A 14
Hulton Cl. CM3: Bor 4F 9
Humber Rd. CM1: Spr 7H 7
CM8: Wthm 4F 23
Hunnable Rd. CM7: Brain 4E 4
Hunt Av. CM9: H'bri 2J 25
Hunt Cl. CO5: Fee 5C 26
Hunter Dr. CM7: Brain 5J 5
Hunters Way CM1: Spr 5A 8
Hunt's Cl. CM1: Writ 5F 11
Hunt's Dr. CM1: Writ 5F 11
Hurrell Down CM3: Bor 3G 9
Hurrells La. CM3: Lit B 2A 14
Hurst Way CM2: Spr 3F 13
Hutley Cl. CM8: Wthm 6K 23
Hyacinth Ct. CM1: Spr 5K 7
Hyde Farm Chase CM3: Dan 2K 21
Hyde Grn. CM3: Dan 6K 15
Hyde La. CM3: Dan 6J 15
Hylands Golf Course 4F 17
Hylands House 1H 17
Hylands Pde. CM2: Chelm 7A 12
Hylands Pk. 7G 11
Hythe, The CM9: Mal 5J 25
Hythe Cl. CM7: Bock 1E 4

I

Ickworth Cl. CM77: Gt Not 1B 4
INGATESTONE 4C 24
Ingatestone By-Pass CM4: Inga, Marg 5A 24
Ingatestone Hall 5D 24
Ingatestone Station (Rail) 4D 24
Ingelrica Av. CM3: Hat P 2K 9
Ingram M. CM7: Brain 7H 5
Inkerpole Pl. CM2: Spr 1F 13
Inworth Rd. CO5: Fee 5D 26
Iris Cl. CM1: Spr 7A 8
Isaac Sq. CM2: Gt B 7H 13
Ishams Chase CM8: Wthm 7K 23
Ivy Barn La. CM4: Marg, Mill G 5A 16

J

Jacaranda Cl. CM1: Spr 6A 8
Jackson Pl. CM2: Gt B 7D 12
Jacksons Ct. CM2: Gt B 7G 13
Jacquard Way CM7: Brain 5G 5
Jaggard's Rd. CO6: Cogg 1B 26
James Cft. CM2: Gall 4B 18
Janmead CM8: Wthm 3J 23
Jarndyce CM1: Chelm 6E 6
Jarvis Fld. CM3: Lit B 7K 9
Jasmine Cl. CM1: Spr 5K 7
Jay Cl. CM77: Brain 7D 4
Jeffcut Rd. CM2: Spr 3E 12
Jeffery Rd. CM2: Gt B 6G 13
Jellicoe Way CM7: Brain 3J 5
Jenner Cl. CM7: Brain 6F 5
Jenner Mead CM2: Spr 2G 13
Jennings Pl. CM4: Marg 6E 16
Jersey Rd. CM9: Mal 6J 25
Jersey Way CM7: Brain 5D 4
Jigger Gdns. CM3: Lit W 2K 7
John English Av. CM7: Brain 3E 4
John Henry Keene Memorial Homes CM1: Chelm 1F 27 (1A 12)
John Raven Ct. CO5: Fee 6C 26
John Ray St. CM7: Brain 4H 5
Johnson Cl. CM7: Brain 7F 5
Johnson Rd. CM2: Gt B 1G 19
Johnston Way CM9: Mal 7H 25
Joseph Clibbon Dr. CM1: Spr 4K 7
Jubilee Av. CM1: Broom 2F 7
Jubilee Ct. CM6: Gt Dun 3B 22
Jubilee Ri. CM3: Dan 7J 15
Jubilee Ter. CM1: Chelm 7F 7
Judge Rd. CM2: Spr 1H 13
Julian Cl. CM1: Broom 3G 7
Julien Ct. Rd. CM7: Brain 3G 5
Juniper Ct. CM6: Gt Dun 3A 22
Juniper Cres. CM8: Wthm 2J 23
Juniper Dr. CM2: Chelm 7B 12
Juniper Rd. CM3: Bor 4F 9
Jutland Ho. *CM6: Gt Dun 4C 22 (off White Hart Way)*
Juvina Cl. CM8: Wthm 7H 23

K

Keats Av. CM7: Brain 7F 5
Keats Cl. CM9: Mal 7H 25
Keeble Pk. CM9: Mal 7G 25
Keeble Way CM7: Brain 4G 5
Keene Way CM2: Gall 3B 18
KELVEDON 6B 26
Kelvedon Cl. CM1: Chelm 6F 7
KELVEDON NORTH INTERCHANGE 4E 26
Kelvedon Rd. CO5: Inw 7E 26
CO6: Cogg 4B 26
Kelvedon Station (Rail) 6B 26
Kennet Way CM1: Chelm 7C 6
Kent Gdns. CM7: Brain 3H 5
Kentings, The CM7: Brain 5E 4
Kenworthy Rd. CM7: Brain 5E 4
Kerby Ri. CM2: Spr 3F 13
Kerridge Cl. CM6: Gt Dun 4C 22
Kestrel M. CM9: Mal 7J 25
Kestrel Wlk. CM2: Chelm 2B 18
Ketleys CM2: Gall 3C 18
Keyes Way CM7: Brain 3J 5
Kidder Rd. CM77: Rayne 6A 4
Killegrews CM4: Marg 3G 17
King Charles Ct. CM2: Chelm 7G 27
King Edward Ct. CM1: Chelm 2F 27 (2A 12)
King Edward Way CM8: Wthm 6G 23
Kingfisher Cl. CM9: H'bri 2K 25
Kingfisher Ga. CM7: Brain 2G 5
Kingfisher Lodge CM2: Gt B 6F 13
Kingfishers CM4: Inga 3D 24
Kingfisher Way CO5: K'dn 7B 26
King George Ct. CM2: Chelm 7G 27 (4B 12)
King George's Pl. *CM9: Mal 5H 25 (off High St.)*
Kings Acre CO6: Cogg 2B 26
Kings Chase CM8: Wthm 5J 23
Kings Ct. CM6: Gt Dun 3C 22
Kingsdale Ind. Est., The CM1: Chelm 2J 27 (2C 12)
Kingsford Dr. CM2: Spr 2G 13
Kings Gdns. CO5: Fee 5D 26
Kings Head Wlk. CM2: Chelm 5J 27
Kingsmead Cvn. Pk. CM7: Brain 3J 5
Kings Mdw. Ct. CO5: K'dn 6B 26
Kingsmead Pk. CM7: Brain 3J 5
King's Rd. CM7: Brain 2E 4
Kings Rd. CM1: Chelm 1K 11
Kingston Av. CM2: Chelm 2E 12
Kingston Chase CM9: H'bri 2G 25
Kingston Cres. CM2: Chelm 2E 12
Kings Twr. CM1: Chelm 3F 27
King St. CM9: Mal 6H 25
Kinloch Chase CM8: Wthm 7H 23
Kipling Cl. CM1: Chelm 7F 7
Kipling Way CM7: Brain 7G 5
Kirklees CM1: Chelm 1K 11
Kirkmans Rd. CM2: Gall 3D 18
Kirk Pl. CM2: Spr 2F 13
Kitchen Fld. CM7: Brain 4K 5
Kittiwake Dr. CM9: H'bri 2K 25
Knapton Cl. CM1: Spr 5J 7
Knights Rd. CM7: Brain 6K 5
CO6: Cogg 2B 26
Knights Way CM6: Gt Dun 3C 22
Knox Cl. CM9: Mal 7H 25
Kynaston Pl. CM8: Wthm 4K 23

L

Laburnham Rd. CM6: Gt Dun 3A 22
Laburnum Dr. CM2: Chelm 7B 12
Laburnum Way CM3: Hat P 2J 9
CM8: Wthm 1J 23
Lady La. CM2: Chelm 7H 27 (5B 12)
Ladywell La. CM2: Gt B 1H 19
Lake Mead CM9: H'bri 4K 25
Lakes Ind. Pk. CM7: Brain 5H 5
Lakes Mdw. CO6: Cogg 2C 26
Lakes Rd. CM7: Brain 5H 5
Lakin Cl. CM2: Spr 2G 13
Lamberts Orchard CM7: Brain 3D 4
Lambourne Chase CM2: Gt B 7D 12
Lambourne Gro. CM9: Mal 7G 25
Lammas Dr. CM7: Brain 4K 5
Lancaster Way CM7: Brain 3E 4
Landers Ct. CM1: Chelm 6D 6
Landisdale CM3: Dan 6J 15
Langdale CM77: Gt Not 1B 4
Langdale Gdns. CM2: Chelm 5C 12
Langford Meads CM9: H'bri 1G 25
Langford Rd. CM9: H'bri 1F 25
Langton Av. CM1: Chelm 7D 6
Lapwing Dr. CM9: H'bri 2K 25
CO5: K'dn 7C 26
Larches, The CM3: Bor 4F 9
Larch Gro. CM2: Chelm 7C 12
CM8: Wthm 1J 23
Larch Wlk. *CM3: Hat P 1J 9 (off Rookery Cl.)*
CM9: H'bri, Mal 1K 25
Larch Way CM6: Gt Dun 3A 22
Lark Ri. CM9: H'bri 2K 25
Larkspur Cl. CM8: Wthm 2G 23
Larkspur Ct. CM1: Spr 6A 8
Lathcoates Cres. CM2: Gt B 5E 12
Laurel Dr. CM6: Gt Dun 3A 22
Laurel Gro. CM2: Chelm 5A 12
Laurels, The CM7: Brain 4G 5
CM77: Brain 7C 4
Laurence Av. CM8: Wthm 6J 23
Laurence Cft. CM1: Writ 4F 11
Lavender Cl. CM8: Wthm 2G 23
Lavender Ct. CM1: Spr 7A 8
Lawford La. CM1: Chelm, Writ 2H 11
Lawling Av. CM9: H'bri 2K 25
Lawn Chase CM8: Wthm 5H 23
Lawn La. CM1: Spr 5J 7
Lawns, The CM1: Spr 7J 7
Lawrence Pl. *CM9: Mal 5G 25 (off White Horse La.)*
Leach Cl. CM2: Gt B 6H 13
Lea Cl. CM7: Brain 6K 5
Leapingwell Cl. CM2: Spr 2G 13
Leas, The CM4: Inga 5B 24
Leather La. *CM7: Brain 4F 5 (off Swan Side)*
Lee Ct. CM2: Gt B 6E 12
Leeford CM1: Chelm 6E 6
Leeway, The CM3: Dan 6H 15
Legg St. CM1: Chelm 3H 27 (2B 12)
Leighams Rd. CM3: B'acre, E Han 7G 21
Leonard M. CM7: Brain 7H 5
Leslie Newnham Ct. CM9: Mal 6H 25
Levens Way CM77: Gt Not 2B 4
Lewin Pl. CM3: Bor 4F 9
Lewis Ct. CM6: Gt Dun 3C 22
Lewis Dr. CM2: Chelm 7B 12
Ley, The CM7: Brain 6K 5
Leybourne Dr. CM1: Spr 5J 7
Leyfields CM77: Rayne 6A 4
Leys, The CM2: Spr 7A 8
Leywood Cl. CM7: Brain 5K 5
Lichfield Cl. CM1: Chelm 1J 11
Lie Fld. Cl. CM7: Brain 4K 5
Lifchild Cl. CM8: Wthm 7J 23
Lilac Cl. CM2: Chelm 7C 12
Lily Cl. CM1: Spr 6A 8
Limbourne Dr. CM9: H'bri 2K 25
Limebrook Way CM9: Mal 7F 25
Lime Cl. CM8: Wthm 1J 23
Limes, The CM2: Gall 4B 18
CM4: Inga 4D 24
Lime Tree Cotts. CM6: Gt Dun 2C 22
Lime Tree Hill CM6: Gt Dun 2C 22
Lime Wlk. CM2: Chelm 7B 12
LINDEN CENTRE 1E 6
Linden Cl. CM2: Chelm 6C 12
Lindens, The CM7: Brain 6G 5
Lindisfarne Ct. CM9: Mal 7F 25
Linfold Cl. CM7: Brain 3K 5
Linford M. CM9: Mal 7F 25
Lingwood Cl. CM3: Dan 6G 15
Lingwood Common Nature Reserve 5F 15
Links Dr. CM2: Wid 6K 11
Linnet Dr. CM2: Chelm 1A 18
Linnett Ter. CM9: H'bri 2J 25
Lintons, The CM2: Sando 7K 13
Lionfield Ter. CM1: Spr 2D 12
Lister Rd. CM7: Brain 7F 5
Lister Tye CM2: Chelm 6C 12
Litchborough Pk. CM3: Lit B 5H 15
Littell Tweed CM2: Spr 2G 13
Lit. and Gt. Sir Hughes La. CM2: Gt B 4G 19
LITTLE BADDOW 1F 15
Lit. Baddow Rd. CM3: Dan 6G 15
CM9: Lit B, Wdhm W 2J 15
Lit. Braxted La. CM8: L Brax, Riven 3K 23
LITTLE COMMON 7A 4
Little Dorrit CM1: Chelm 5D 6
Little Flds. CM3: Dan 6J 15
Lit. Hyde La. CM4: Fry, Inga 1C 24
Lit. Hyde Rd. CM4: Inga 1E 24
LITTLE LONDON 5D 26
Lit. Meadow CM1: Writ 4E 10
Little Nell CM1: Chelm 5D 6
Little Orchards CM1: Broom 5G 7
CO5: K'dn 7A 26
LITTLE OXNEY GREEN 5C 10
Lit. Pasture Cl. CM7: Brain 3E 4

Little Sq. CM7: Brain 4F 5
(off Swan Side)
Little Stile CM1: Writ 5E 10
Lit. Waltham Rd. CM1: Spr 3J 7
Llewellyn Cl. CM1: Spr 2D 12
Lobelia Cl. CM1: Spr 6B 8
Lockram La. CM8: Wthm 4H 23
(Guithavon Valley)
CM8: Wthm 4J 23
(Newlands Dr.)
Lockside Marina
CM2: Chelm 4D 12
Lodge Av. CM2: Gt B 6F 13
Lodge Cres. CM3: Bor 5F 9
Lodge Rd. CM1: Writ 5D 10
CM3: B'acre 7G 21
CM7: Brain 6F 5
CM9: Mal 4G 25
Lodge Va. CM1: Spr 3K 7
Loftin Way CM2: Gt B 6D 12
Lombardy Pl.
CM1: Chelm 2G 27 (2B 12)
London Rd. CM2: Wid 7J 11
CM7: Brain, Gt Not 7E 4
(not continuous)
CM8: K'dn, Riven 2K 23
CM9: Mal 4F 25
CM77: Blk N, Brain, Gt Not
3B 4
CO5: Fee 5D 26
CO5: K'dn 7A 26
Lonebarn Link CM2: Spr 7C 8
Longacre CM1: Chelm 5H 11
Long Acres CM7: Brain 6G 5
Long Brandocks CM1: Writ 4D 10
Long Comn. CM9: H'bri 2G 25
Longfellow Rd. CM9: Mal 6H 25
Longfield CM8: Wthm 1G 23
CM9: Mal 6H 25
Longfield Rd. CM2: Gt B 6E 12
Longfields CM9: Mal 5H 25
Long Grn. CM77: Cres 7K 5
Long La. CM77: Rayne 7A 4
Longleaf Dr. CM7: Brain 7F 5
Longleat Cl. CM1: Chelm 5E 6
Longmead Av. CM2: Gt B 5F 13
Long Mdw. CM77: Gt Not 3A 4
Longmeads Cl. CM1: Writ 4E 10
Longmore Av. CM2: Gt B 5E 12
Longship Way CM9: Mal 7F 25
Longshots Cl. CM1: Broom 3F 7
Longstomps Av. CM2: Chelm 7A 12
Lordship Rd. CM1: Writ 3F 11
Louvain Dr. CM1: Spr 5A 8
Loves Wlk. CM1: Writ 5F 11
CM2: Gt B 6E 12
Lovibond Pl. CM2: Spr 1F 13
Lwr. Anchor St.
CM2: Chelm 6F 27 (4A 12)
Lwr. Chapel Hill CM7: Brain 5H 5
LOWER GREEN 7J 13
Lower Grn. CM2: Gall 5B 18
Lower King CM7: Brain 6K 5
Lwr. Mill Fld. CM6: Gt Dun 5D 22
Luard Way CM8: Wthm 5H 23
Lucas Av. CM2: Chelm 7C 12
Lucerne Way CM1: Writ 5F 11
Lucksfield Way CM2: Gt B 1F 19
Ludgores La. CM3: Dan 1F 21
Ludham Hall La. CM77: Brain 1C 4
Lukin's Dr. CM6: Gt Dun 5C 22
Lupin Dr. CM1: Spr 6A 8
Lupin M. CM1: Spr 6A 8
Lyndhurst Dr. CM3: B'acre 5H 21
Lynmouth Av.
CM2: Chelm 7J 27 (5C 12)
Lynmouth Gdns.
CM2: Chelm 7J 27 (4C 12)
Lynton Dr. CM1: Spr 7K 7
Lyon Cl. CM2: Gall 3B 18
Lyons Ct. CM1: Spr 7K 7
Lyster Av. CM2: Gt B 6G 13

M

Mace Av. CM7: Brain 4D 4
Mace Wlk. CM1: Chelm 2K 11
Macmillan Ct.
CM2: Chelm 7H 27 (4B 12)
Madeline Pl. CM1: Chelm 6D 6
Madison Heights 6K 25
Maeldune Heritage Cen. (Mus.)
4H 25
Magistrates' Court
Chelmsford 4H 27
Magnolia Cl. CM2: Chelm 7B 12
CM8: Wthm 1J 23
Magwitch Cl. CM1: Chelm 5E 6
Maidment Cres. CM8: Wthm 6H 23
Main Rd. CM1: Broom 5G 7
CM2: Sando 6B 14
CM3: B'acre, Wdhm F 5H 21
CM3: Bor 5D 8
CM3: Broom, Chelm, Lit W
5G 7
CM3: Dan 6F 15
CM3: E Han 7D 20
CM4: Marg 6D 16
Makemores CM77: Rayne 5A 4
MALDON 4G 25
Maldon District Mus. 5J 25
Maldon Embroidery 4H 25
(off Market Hill)
Maldon Golf Course 2F 25
Maldon Moot Hall 4G 25
Maldon (Park & Ride) 3H 25
Maldon Rd.
CM2: Gt B, Sando 6F 13
CM3: Dan 6H 15
(Gay Bowers La.)
CM3: Dan 2K 21
(Hyde La.)
CM3: Hat P 1J 9
CM4: Marg 6E 16
CM8: W Bis, Wthm 5J 23
CM9: L'frd 1F 25
CO5: K'dn 7A 26
Maldon Yacht Club 5J 25
Mall, The CM77: Brain 7D 4
Mallard Cl. CM77: Gt Not 3B 4
CO5: K'dn 6B 26
Mallard Rd. CM2: Chelm 1A 18
Mallows, The CM9: Mal 7H 25
Maltese Rd. CM1: Chelm 2A 12
Maltings, The CM6: Gt Dun 3C 22
CM77: Rayne 5A 4
Maltings Chase CM4: Inga 4C 24
Maltings Ct. CM8: Wthm 6H 23
Maltings La. CM8: Wthm 6G 23
Maltings Rd. CM2: Gt B 1G 19
Maltings Vw. CM7: Brain 4G 5
Malvern Cl. CM1: Chelm 6C 6
Malyon Cl. CM7: Brain 4D 4
Malyon Rd. CM8: Wthm 6H 23
Mandeville Way CM1: Broom 1G 7
Manor Dr. CM2: Gt B 6F 13
Manor Rd.
CM2: Chelm 7H 27 (4B 12)
CM8: Wthm 2J 23
Manor St. CM7: Brain 4F 5
Manse Chase CM9: Mal 6H 25
Manse Gdns. CM6: Gt Dun 4C 22
Mansfields CM1: Writ 4D 10
Maple Av. CM7: Brain 5D 4
CM9: H'bri 1K 25
Maple Dr. CM2: Chelm 7B 12
CM8: Wthm 1J 23
Maple Way CM6: Gt Dun 3A 22
Marconi Athletic & Social Club
7E 12
Marconi Plaza
CM1: Chelm 3F 27 (3A 12)
Marconi Rd.
CM1: Chelm 2G 27 (2B 12)
Margaret's Ho. CO5: K'dn 7B 26
MARGARETTING 6E 16
Margaretting Rd. CM1: Writ 2E 16
CM2: Chelm, Gall 5K 17
MARGARETTING TYE 7G 17
Marigold Cl. CM1: Spr 6A 8
Marina Rd. CM3: Hat P 1J 9
Mariners Way CM9: Mal 7H 25
Market End CO6: Cogg 2B 26
Market Hill CM9: Mal 4H 25
CO6: Cogg 2C 26
Market La. CM8: Wthm 7K 23
Market Pl. CM4: Inga 3C 24
CM6: Gt Dun 3C 22
CM7: Brain 4F 5
Market Rd.
CM1: Chelm 4G 27 (3B 12)
Market Sq.
CM1: Chelm 5G 27 (3B 12)
Market St. CM7: Brain 4F 5
Markland Cl. CM2: Gall 3C 18
Markland Dr. CM9: Mal 6F 25
Marks Cl. CM4: Inga 6A 24
Marks Gdns. CM7: Brain 4J 5
MARKS RDBT. 4K 5
Marlborough Rd.
CM2: Chelm 7F 27 (5A 12)
CM7: Brain 3H 5
Marlborough Ter.
CM2: Chelm 7F 27 (4A 12)
Marlowe Cl. CM7: Brain 7G 5
CM9: Mal 7H 25
Marney Cl. CM2: Gt B 5E 12
Marshall Cl. CO5: Fee 5C 26
Marshalls Dr. CM7: Brain 6E 4
Marshalls Rd. CM7: Brain 6E 4
Marsh La. CM13: Mount 7B 24
Marston Beck CM2: Spr 3G 13
Martens Mdw. CM7: Brain 4K 5
Martingale Dr. CM1: Spr 5A 8
Marvens CM2: Gall 3D 18
Mary Munnion Quarter
CM2: Chelm 6K 11
Mascalls, The CM2: Gt B 5E 12
Mascalls Way CM2: Gt B 5E 12
Masefield Rd. CM7: Brain 7F 5
CM9: Mal 7H 25
Mashbury Rd. CM1: Chig J 4A 6
Matfield Cl. CM1: Spr 5J 7
Mayes La. CM2: Sando 7A 14
CM3: Dan 7G 15
Mayfield Rd. CM1: Writ 4E 10
Mayflower Dr. CM9: Mal 7H 25
Mayland Cl. CM9: H'bri 3K 25
Mayland Ho. CM8: Wthm 4J 23
Mayland Rd. CM8: Wthm 4J 23
Maylands Dr. CM77: Brain 7D 4
Maynard Cl. CM6: Gt Dun 3C 22
Mayne Crest CM1: Spr 5K 7
Maypole Rd. CM9: H'bri 1G 25
Maysent Av. CM7: Brain 2F 5
May Wlk. CM2: Chelm 6C 12
Mazers Ct. CM7: Brain 5F 5
Mead, The CM6: Gt Dun 2B 22
Meades, The
CM2: Chelm 6F 27 (4A 12)
Meadgate Av. CM2: Gt B 5D 12
Meadgate Ter.
CM2: Gt B 7K 27 (5D 12)
Meadow Bank CM3: Hat P 1H 9
Meadow Brown Ct. CM7: Brain 6E 4
Meadow Pk. CM7: Brain 7E 4
Meadows, The CM1: Chelm 5J 27
Meadowside
CM1: Chelm 2G 27 (2B 12)
CM2: Chelm 3K 27 (2C 12)
CM7: Brain 2E 4
Meadows Shop. Cen., The
CM2: Chelm 5J 27 (3C 12)
Meadow Vw. CM3: B'acre 5G 21
Meadow Wlk.
CM1: Chelm 5J 27 (3C 12)
Mead Path CM2: Chelm 5K 11
Meads, The CM4: Inga 3C 24
Meads Cl. CM4: Inga 3C 24
Meadway CM9: Mal 6J 25
Mearns Pl. CM2: Spr 1F 13
Medlar Cl. CM8: Wthm 2J 23
Medley Rd. CM77: Rayne 5A 4
Medway Av. CM8: Wthm 4F 23
Medway Cl. CM1: Chelm 1H 11
Meeson Mdws. CM9: Mal 7F 25
Meggy Tye CM2: Spr 1H 13
Megs Way CM7: Brain 5H 5
Melba Ct. CM1: Writ 4G 11
Melbourne Av. CM1: Chelm 7C 6
Melbourne Ct. CM1: Chelm 7D 6
Melbourne Pde. CM1: Chelm 7D 6
Melbourne Stadium 6D 6
Melford Gro. CM77: Gt Not 1A 4
Mellings CO6: Cogg 1B 26
Mellish Gro. CM6: Gt Dun 2C 22
Mellor Cl. CM4: Inga 3C 24
Memory Cl. CM9: Mal 7H 25
Mendip Pl. CM1: Chelm 6C 6
Mendip Rd. CM1: Chelm 6C 6
Menish Way CM2: Spr 2G 13
Meon Cl. CM1: Spr 6H 7
Mercia Cl. CM2: Gt B 1G 19
Mercury Pl. CM9: H'bri 2G 25
Merdle Sq. CM1: Chelm 6E 6
Merks Hill CM6: Gt Dun 2E 22
Merlin Pl. CM1: Chelm 7E 6
Mermaid Way CM9: Mal 7J 25
Mersea Fleet Way CM7: Brain 6J 5
Mersey Rd. CM8: Wthm 4G 23
Mersey Way CM1: Chelm 7B 6
Meteor Way CM1: Chelm 3K 11
Mews Ct.
CM2: Chelm 7G 27 (4B 12)
Micawber Way CM1: Chelm 5C 6
Middleditch Ct.
CM1: Chelm 4F 27 (3A 12)
Middle King CM7: Brain 6K 5
Midguard Way CM9: Mal 7G 25
Milbank CM2: Spr 1H 13
Milburn Cres. CM1: Chelm 4H 11
Mildmay Ct. CM2: Chelm 6H 27
Mildmay Rd.
CM2: Chelm 7H 27 (5B 12)
Mildmays CM3: Dan 5E 14
Mildmay Sports Hall 7G 7
Mildmay Wlk.
CM2: Chelm 7H 27 (4B 12)
Millar, The CM1: Broom 1F 7
Millbridge Rd. CM8: Wthm 4H 23
Mill Ct. CM6: Gt Dun 4C 22
(off Mill La.)
CM7: Brain 5H 5
Millennium Gdns.
Maldon 4H 25
(off Market Hill)
Millennium Way
CM7: Brain, Tye G 5H 5
Millers Cft. CM2: Gt B 7F 13
CM6: Gt Dun 3D 22
Millers Dr. CM77: Gt Not 1B 4
Millers Gdns. CO5: K'dn 7A 26
Millers Mead CO5: Fee 5D 26
Millers M. CM4: Inga 3D 24
Millfields CM1: Writ 4E 10
CM3: Dan 7J 15
MILL GREEN 1A 24
Mill Grn. Rd.
CM4: Fry, Mill G 1A 24
Mill Hill CM2: Gall 4K 17
CM7: Brain 5H 5
Milligans Chase CM2: Gall 5B 18
Mill La.
CM1: Broom, Chelm, Spr 3G 7
CM3: Dan 7H 15
CM3: Lit B 2G 15
CM4: Mill G 1B 24
CM6: Gt Dun 4C 22
CM8: Wthm 5H 23
CM9: Mal 4G 25
Mill Pk. Dr. CM7: Brain 6H 5
Mill Rd. CM9: Mal 5J 25
Millson Bank CM2: Spr 1G 13
Mill Va. Lodge CM8: Wthm 4H 23
(off Guithavon St.)
Mill Vue Rd. CM2: Spr 3F 13
Milton Av. CM7: Brain 7G 5
Milton Pl. CM1: Chelm 7E 6
Milton Rd. CM8: Wthm 1H 23
CM9: Mal 7H 25
Mimosa Cl. CM1: Spr 6A 8
Minster Way CM9: Mal 7F 25
Mirosa Dr. CM9: Mal 6J 25
Mirosa Reach CM9: Mal 7H 25
Mitton Va. CM2: Spr 3F 13
Moat Farm Chase
CM8: Wthm 3H 23
Molrams La. CM2: Gt B 7H 13
Monkdowns Rd.
CO6: Cogg 1D 26
Monks Ct. CM8: Wthm 3G 23
Monks Mead CM3: B'acre 4H 21
Montagu Gdns. CM1: Spr 5A 8
Montfort Dr. CM2: Gt B 7E 12
Montgomery Cl. CM1: Spr 5K 7
Montrose Rd. CM2: Spr 1F 13
Moores Bri. La. CM3: Dan 6G 15
Moorfield Ct. CM8: Wthm 5H 23
Moor Hall La.
CM3: Dan, E Han 5G 21
Moorings, The CM9: Mal 4H 25
Moors Cft. CM7: Brain 4K 5
Moran Av. CM1: Chelm 5G 7
Moretons CM2: Gall 4B 18
Morrison Dr. CM8: Wthm 7H 23
Morris Rd. CM2: Chelm 3D 12
Mortimer Rd. CM3: Hat P 1J 9
Mortimer Way CM8: Wthm 7G 23
Moss Path CM2: Gall 3C 18
Moss Rd. CM8: Wthm 3K 23
Moss Wlk. CM2: Chelm 7B 12
Motts Cl. CM7: Brain 3E 4
Motts La. CM8: Wthm 2J 23
MOULSHAM 4B 12
Moulsham Barn CM2: Chelm 6C 12

Moulsham Chase
CM2: Chelm 5C 12
Moulsham Dr. CM2: Chelm 5B 12
Moulsham Mill Cen.
CM2: Chelm 7K 27 (4D 12)
Moulsham St.
CM2: Chelm 7F 27 (5A 12)
Moulsham Thrift CM2: Chelm . . .7A 12
Mountbatten Rd. CM7: Brain 3H 5
Mountbatten Way CM1: Spr 5J 7
Mounthill Av. CM2: Chelm 2D 12
MOUNTNESSING 7A 24
Mountnessing Rd. CM12: Bill . . .7E 24
Mountney Cl. CM4: Inga 6A 24
Mt. Pleasant CM9: Mal 5G 25
Mount Rd. CM7: Brain 4G 5
CO6: Cogg 2D 26
Mowden Hall La. CM3: Hat P 3K 9
Mulberries, The CM7: Brain 5G 5
(off South St.)
Mulberry Gdns. CM8: Wthm 2J 23
Mulberry Way CM1: Spr 7J 7
Mullins Rd. CM7: Bock 1F 5
Multon Lea CM1: Spr 5B 8
Mundon Rd. CM7: Brain 6K 5
CM9: Mal 6H 25
Munro Rd. CM8: Wthm 1H 23
Murchison Cl. CM1: Chelm 7D 6
Murray Cl. CM7: Bock 1F 5
Murrell Lock CM2: Spr 1G 13
Mynards Way CM3: Dan 6E 14
Myneer Pk. CO6: Cogg 2D 26

N

Nabbott Rd. CM1: Chelm 3J 11
Nalla Gdns. CM1: Chelm 6F 7
Namco Funscape
Braintree 7J 5
Nancy Edwards Pl.
CM1: Chelm 2K 11
Napier Ct. CM1: Chelm 7D 6
Narvik Cl. CM9: Mal 7F 25
Nash Dr. CM1: Broom 1F 7
Nathan's La.
CM1: E Com, Writ 1A 16
Navigation Pl. CM9: H'bri 3J 25
Navigation Rd.
CM2: Chelm 4K 27 (3C 12)
Navigation Yd.
CM2: Chelm 4K 27 (3C 12)
Nayling Rd. CM7: Brain 5C 4
Nelson Cres. CM9: Mal 7J 25
Nelson Gdns. CM7: Brain 3J 5
Nelson Gro. CM1: Chelm 2K 11
Ness Wlk. CM8: Wthm 4F 23
New Bowers Way CM1: Spr 6K 7
New Ct. Pl. CM2: Chelm 2E 12
New Ct. Rd. CM2: Chelm 2D 12
New Dukes Way CM2: Spr 1F 13
New England Cl. CM3: B'acre . . .5H 21
Newland Grove Nature Reserve
. . . . .2H 7
Newland Pl. CM8: Wthm 5J 23
Newlands Dr. CM8: Wthm 4J 23
Newlands Shop. Cen., The
CM8: Wthm 4J 23
Newland St. CM8: Wthm 5H 23
New Lodge Chase CM3: Lit B . . .2D 14
New London Rd.
CM2: Chelm 7F 27 (5A 12)
New Nabbotts Way CM1: Spr 5K 7
NEWNEY GREEN 3A 10
Newnham Cl. CM7: Brain 5E 4
Newnham Grn. CM9: Mal 4F 25
Newport Cl. CM2: Gt B 7H 13
New Rd. CM1: Broom 3G 7
CM2: Gt B 7F 13
CM3: Hat P 1J 9
CM4: Inga 2D 24
CM77: Rayne 6A 4
CO5: K'dn 7A 26
New St. CM1: Chelm . . .1H 27 (3B 12)
CM6: Gt Dun 4C 22
CM7: Brain 4F 5
(not continuous)
CM9: Mal 5G 25
New St. Flds. CM6: Gt Dun 4C 22
New St. Pas. CM6: Gt Dun 4C 22
(off New St.)
Newton Cl. CM7: Brain 6F 5
Newton Grn. CM6: Gt Dun 3B 22
Newton Gro. CM6: Gt Dun 3A 22
Newton Hall Chase
CM6: Gt Dun 2A 22
NEWTOWN 5B 26
New Writtle St.
CM2: Chelm 6F 27 (4A 12)
Nicholas Cl. CM1: Writ 4F 11
Nicholas Ct. CM1: Chelm 6C 6
CM8: Wthm 4H 23
Nichols Gro. CM7: Brain 4H 5
Nicholson Pl. CM3: E Han 7D 20
Nickleby Rd. CM1: Chelm 5C 6
Nightingale Cl. CM8: Wthm 6G 23
Nightingale Cnr. CM9: Mal 6H 25
(off Fambridge Rd.)
Nineacres CM7: Brain 6G 5
Noakes Av. CM2: Gt B 1E 18
Norfolk Cl. CM9: Mal 6F 25
Norfolk Dr. CM1: Chelm 5F 7
Norfolk Gdns. CM7: Brain 3H 5
Norfolk Rd. CM9: Mal 6F 25
Normandy Way CM7: Brain 1F 5
Normansfield CM6: Gt Dun 5D 22
Norris Cl. CM7: Brain 2J 5
Northampton Cl. CM7: Brain 2K 5
North Av. CM1: Chelm 7E 6
North Ct. CM4: Inga 3D 24
(off Summerfields)
North Ct. Rd. CM1: Broom 1F 7
North Dell CM1: Spr 5J 7
North Dr. CM2: Gt B 6F 13
Northey Vw. CM9: H'bri 3K 25
North Hill CM3: Lit B 6K 9, 1F 15
North St. CM6: Gt Dun 3C 22
CM9: Mal 5J 25
Northumberland Cl.
CM7: Brain 3H 5
Northumberland Ct.
CM2: Spr 1F 13
Norton Rd. CM1: Chelm 2A 12
CM4: Inga 3C 24
Notley Cross CM77: Brain 7D 4
Notley Grn. CM77: Gt Not 2A 4
Notley Rd.
CM7: Blk N, Brain, Gt Not . . .5F 5
Notley Sports Cen. 7F 5
Nottage Cres. CM7: Brain 4E 4
Nuffield Health
Chelmsford 2K 27 (2C 12)
Nunns Cl. CO6: Cogg 2C 26
Nursery Dr. CM7: Brain 2G 5
Nursery La. CM3: Dan 5H 15
Nursery Ri. CM6: Gt Dun 5C 22
Nursery Rd.
CM2: Chelm 7G 27 (5B 12)

O

Oak Bungs. CM7: Brain 4E 4
Oak Cl. CM9: Mal 7J 25
Oak Cotts. CM3: Bor 4F 9
Oak Fall CM8: Wthm 1J 23
Oak Ind. Pk. CM6: Gt Dun 5E 22
Oaklands Cl. CM77: Brain 7D 4
Oaklands Cres. CM2: Chelm 5B 12
Oaklands Way CM3: Lit B 3G 15
Oaklea Av. CM2: Chelm 1E 12
Oakley Rd. CM7: Bock 1F 5
Oak Lodge Tye CM1: Spr 6B 8
Oak Rd. CM9: H'bri 1J 25
Oakroyd Av. CM6: Gt Dun 4D 22
Oakroyd Ho. CM6: Gt Dun 4D 22
Oak Tree Gdns. CM7: Brain 1F 5
Oasis Ct. CM2: Spr 7A 8
Oast Ho. Spinney CM7: Bock 1F 5
Oat Leys CM1: Chelm 4E 6
Observer Way CO5: K'dn 5B 26
Ockelford Av. CM1: Chelm 7E 6
Octavia Dr. CM8: Wthm 6G 23
Odeon Cinema
Chelmsford 6J 27 (3C 12)
Okeley CM1: Chelm 1A 12
Oldbury Av. CM2: Gt B 6F 13
Old Church Rd. CM3: E Han 7D 20
CM13: Bill, Mount 7A 24
Old Ct. CM1: Spr 2D 12
Old Ct. Rd. CM2: Chelm 2D 12
Old Court Theatre
Chelmsford 2D 12
Old Forge Rd. CM3: Bor 4F 9
Old Mill Cl. CM9: Mal 4H 25
Old Orchard, The
CM2: Howe G 4K 19
Old Roxwell Rd. CM1: Writ 1D 10
Old St Michaels Dr.
CM7: Brain 4E 4
Old School Ct. CM3: Hat P 1K 9
Old School Fld. CM1: Spr 1E 12
Old Southend Rd.
CM2: Howe G 5K 19
Oliver Cl. CM9: H'bri 3J 25
Oliver Pl. CM8: Wthm 4K 23
Olivers Dr. CM8: Wthm 7H 23
Oliver Way CM1: Chelm 6D 6
Oliveswood Rd. CM6: Gt Dun . . .5C 22
Ongar Rd. CM1: Coo G, Writ . . .5A 10
CM6: Gt Dun 7A 22
Ongar Rd. Trad. Est.
CM6: Gt Dun 5D 22
Orange Tree Cl. CM2: Chelm 7C 12
Orchard, The CM9: H'bri 2G 25
Orchard Cl. CM1: Writ 4F 11
CM2: Gt B 1C 18
CM3: Hat P 1J 9
CM9: Mal 5G 25
Orchard Dr. CM7: Brain 6G 5
Orchard Rd. CM9: Mal 5G 25
CO5: K'dn 6B 26
Orchards CM8: Wthm 5H 23
Orchard St.
CM2: Chelm 6H 27 (4B 12)
Orchard Wlk. CM9: H'bri 1K 25
(off Chestnut M.)
Orchid Av. CM8: Wthm 2G 23
Orford Cres. CM1: Spr 7H 7
Orion Way CM7: Brain 3H 5
Orton Cl. CM4: Marg 6E 16
Orwell Wlk. CM8: Wthm 3G 23
Osbert Rd. CM8: Wthm 6G 23
Osea Way CM1: Spr 7A 8
Osprey Way CM2: Chelm 1A 18
Ottley Pl. CM4: Marg 6E 16
Ouse Chase CM8: Wthm 4F 23
Owers Rd. CM8: Wthm 7G 23
Oxford Ct. CM2: Spr 1E 12
Oxlip Rd. CM8: Wthm 2G 23
Oxney Ho. CM1: Writ 4D 10
Oxney Mead CM1: Writ 5D 10
Oyster M. CM9: H'bri 2G 25
Oyster Pl. CM2: Spr 1F 13

P

Packe Cl. CO5: Fee 5C 26
Paddock Dr. CM1: Spr 5K 7
Paddocks, The CM4: Inga 4C 24
CM8: Wthm 4J 23
CM77: Rayne 5A 4
PADHAMS GREEN 7C 24
Padham's Grn. Rd.
CM4: Inga 7C 24
Page Cl. CM8: Wthm 6F 23
Paignton Av. CM1: Spr 7J 7
Palm Cl. CM2: Chelm 7C 12
CM8: Wthm 1J 23
Palmers Cft. CM2: Spr 3G 13
Palmerston Lodge CM2: Gt B . . .6F 13
Panfield La. CM7: Brain 3E 4
Panfield Rd. CM7: Brain, Pan 1E 4
Pantile Cl. CM8: Wthm 7J 23
Pantling's La. CO5: K'dn 4A 26
Panton M. CM7: Brain 7G 5
Pan Wlk. CM1: Chelm 7C 6
Parade, The CM1: Chelm 6F 7
Paradise Rd. CM1: Writ 5F 11
Park & Ride
Chelmer Valley 1J 7
Maldon 3H 25
Sandon 5K 13
Park Av. CM1: Chelm 2K 11
Parkdale CM3: Dan 6E 14
Park Dr. CM4: Inga 3D 24
CM7: Brain 7G 5
CM9: Mal 5J 25
Pk. Drive Health Club 6J 25
Parker Rd.
CM2: Chelm 7J 27 (4C 12)
Parkinson Dr. CM1: Chelm 5K 11
Parklands CM7: Brain 7G 5
CO6: Cogg 2C 26
Parklands Dr.
CM1: Spr 3K 27 (2C 12)
Parklands Way CM2: Gall 4C 18
Park Rd.
CM1: Chelm 3G 27 (2B 12)
CM9: Mal 5G 25
Park Vw. Cres. CM2: Gt B 1F 19
Parkway
CM1: Chelm
. . . . .2F 27, 4F 27 (2A 12)
CM2: Chelm 5G 27 (3A 12)
Parnell Pl. CM7: Brain 5G 5
Parr Cl. CM7: Brain 3K 5
Parsonage Cl. CM1: Broom 3F 7
Parsonage Downs
CM6: Gt Dun 1B 22
PARSONAGE GREEN 4E 6
Parsonage La. CM3: Lit B 3F 15
CM4: Marg 7E 16
Partridge Av. CM1: Chelm 6E 6
PARTRIDGE GREEN 1E 6
Partridge Wlk.
CM77: Gt Not 3B 4
Paschal Way CM2: Gt B 5E 12
Pasture Rd. CM8: Wthm 5K 23
Patching Hall La.
CM1: Broom, Chelm 4E 6
Pattison Cl. CM8: Wthm 6J 23
Pavitt Mdw. CM2: Gall 4C 18
Pawle Cl. CM2: Gt B 6G 13
Paycocke's House & Garden . . .3B 26
Paycocke Way CO6: Cogg 1C 26
Payne Cl. CM8: Wthm 7G 23
Payne Pl. CM3: E Han 7D 20
Paynes La. CM3: Bor 4D 8
Peacock Cl. CM7: Brain 6F 5
Pearce Mnr. CM2: Chelm 5K 11
Pearl Dr. CM7: Brain 4J 5
Pearl Sq. CM2: Gt B 7E 12
Pearson Gro. CM1: Spr 1D 12
Peartree Cl. CM7: Brain 6G 5
Peartree La. CM3: Dan 3H 21
Pease Pl. CM3: E Han 7D 20
Pedlars Cl. CM3: Dan 7J 15
Pedlars Path CM3: Dan 7J 15
Peel Cres. CM7: Brain 4E 4
Peel Rd. CM2: Spr 1E 12
Peers Sq. CM2: Spr 1G 13
Pegasus Way CM7: Brain 2E 4
Peggotty Cl. CM1: Chelm 6E 6
Pelly Av. CM8: Wthm 6J 23
Pemberton Av.
CM4: Inga 3C 24
Pemberton Ct. CM4: Inga 3C 24
Pembroke Av. CM9: Mal 6G 25
Pembroke Pl. CM1: Chelm 5G 7
(not continuous)
Penhaligon Ct. CM8: Wthm 4J 23
(off Newlands Dr.)
Pennine Rd. CM1: Chelm 6C 6
Penn M. CM7: Brain 7G 5
Pennyroyal Cres.
CM8: Wthm 2G 23
Penny Royal Rd. CM3: Dan 7F 15
Penny's La. CM4: Marg 6D 16
Penrose Mead CM1: Writ 5F 11
Penshurst Pl. CM77: Gt Not 2A 4
Penticton Rd. CM7: Brain 5D 4
Pentland Av. CM1: Chelm 6F 7
Penzance Cl. CM1: Spr 7K 7
Peregrine Dr. CM2: Chelm 1A 18
Perriclose CM1: Spr 5J 7
Perrin Pl. CM2: Chelm 4A 12
Perryfields CM7: Brain 6F 5
Perry Hill CM1: Spr 2K 27 (2D 12)
Perry Rd. CM8: Wthm 6K 23
Perry Way CM8: Wthm 5K 23
Pertwee Dr. CM2: Gt B 7F 13
Petersfield CM1: Chelm 5G 7
Petrebrook CM2: Spr 2G 13
Petre Cl. CM4: Inga 5B 24
Petrel Way CM2: Chelm 7C 12
Petunia Cres. CM1: Spr 6A 8
Petworth Cl. CM77: Gt Not 1A 4
PHARISEE GREEN 7A 22
Pheasanthouse Wood Nature Reserve
. . . . .3H 15
Philip Rd. CM8: Wthm 6G 23
Philips Cl. CM77: Rayne 5A 4
Philips Rd. CM77: Rayne 5A 4
Phillips Chase CM7: Brain 2G 5
Philpot End La. CM6: Gt Dun . . .7B 22
Phoenix Gro. CM2: Chelm 5A 12
Pickpocket La. CM77: Blk N 2C 4
Pickwick Av. CM1: Chelm 6C 6
Pierrefitte Way CM7: Brain 4E 4
Pilgrim Cl. CM7: Brain 2F 5
Pine Av. CM6: Gt Dun 3A 22
Pine Cl. CM4: Inga 3D 24
Pine Dr. CM4: Inga 3D 24
Pine Gro. CM8: Wthm 1J 23

Pines, The CM3: Hat P . . . 1J **9**
Pines Rd. CM1: Chelm . . . 7C **6**
Pinkham Dr. CM8: Wthm . . . 6H **23**
Pintail Cres. CM77: Gt Not . . . 2B **4**
Pipchin Rd. CM1: Chelm . . . 6E **6**
Piper's Tye CM2: Gall . . . 3D **18**
Pitfield CM2: Gt B . . . 5D **12**
Pitt Av. CM8: Wthm . . . 6J **23**
Pitt Chase CM2: Gt B . . . 1E **18**
Pitt Grn. CM8: Wthm . . . 6J **23**
Plains Fld. CM7: Brain . . . 6K **5**
Plaiters Way CM7: Brain . . . 4K **5**
Plane Tree Cl. CM2: Chelm . . . 7B **12**
Plantation Rd. CM3: Bor . . . 4G **9**
Ploughmans La.
CM77: Gt Not . . . 7C **4**
Plover Wlk. CM2: Chelm . . . 1B **18**
Plume Av. CM9: Mal . . . 6G **25**
Plumptre La. CM3: Dan . . . 1F **21**
Plumtree Av. CM2: Gt B . . . 7F **13**
Plymouth Rd. CM1: Spr . . . 7K **7**
Pochard Way CM77: Gt Not . . . 3B **4**
Pocklington Cl. CM2: Spr . . . 1G **13**
Podsbrook Ho.
CM8: Wthm . . . 4H **23**
Pods Brook Rd.
CM7: Brain, Gt Not . . . 5D **4**
Pollards Grn. CM2: Spr . . . 2F **13**
Pondfield CM6: Gt Dun . . . 3C **22**
Pondholton Dr. CM8: Wthm . . . 7H **23**
Ponds Rd. CM2: Gall . . . 4B **18**
Poor's Piece Nature Reserve
. . . **4H 15**
Popes Leeze CO6: Cogg . . . 2C **26**
Poplar Cl. CM2: Chelm . . . 7C **12**
CM4: Inga . . . 5B **24**
CM8: Wthm . . . 1J **23**
Poplars, The CM6: Gt Dun . . . 2B **22**
Poppy Grn. CM1: Spr . . . 6B **8**
Porters Fld. CM7: Brain . . . 3D **4**
Portland Cl. CM7: Brain . . . 4H **5**
Portreath Pl. CM1: Chelm . . . 5F **7**
Portway CM2: Spr . . . 1H **13**
Postman's La. CM3: Lit B . . . 2G **15**
Postmill Dr. CM7: Brain . . . 4J **5**
Post Office Rd.
CM1: Broom . . . 4G **7**
CM4: Inga . . . 4C **24**
Potters Cl. CM3: Dan . . . 7J **15**
Pottery La. CM1: Chelm . . . 7F **7**
Poulton Cl. CM9: Mal . . . 7H **25**
Pound Flds. CM1: Writ . . . 5F **11**
POWERS HALL END . . . **3G 23**
Powers Hall End CM8: Wthm . . . 3F **23**
Prail Ct. CO6: Cogg . . . 2B **26**
Pratts Farm La. CM3: Lit W . . . 1J **7**
(not continuous)
Primrose Hill CM1: Chelm . . . 2K **11**
Primrose Pl. CM8: Wthm . . . 2G **23**
Primrose Wlk. CM9: Mal . . . 6J **25**
Primula Ct. *CM1: Chelm . . . 2A 12*
(off Primrose Hill)
Primula Way CM1: Spr . . . 6B **8**
Princes Rd. CM2: Chelm . . . 6A **12**
CM9: Mal . . . 5H **25**
Princes St. CM9: Mal . . . 4G **25**
Priors Fld. CM3: B'acre . . . 4H **21**
Priors Way CO6: Cogg . . . 1C **26**
Priory, The CM1: Writ . . . 4F **11**
Priory Cl. CM1: Chelm . . . 3J **11**
Priory Ct. CM3: Hat P . . . 1J **9**
Priory La. CM3: B'acre . . . 4H **21**
CM77: Gt Not . . . 7C **4**
Priory Rd. CM3: B'acre . . . 5G **21**
Private Rd. CM2: Chelm . . . 2H **17**
Progress Ct. CM7: Brain . . . 4E **4**
Prospect Cl. CM3: Hat P . . . 2J **9**
Provident Sq.
CM2: Chelm . . . 5K **27** (3C **12**)
Prykes Dr. CM1: Chelm . . . 3K **11**
Pryor Cl. CM8: Wthm . . . 5J **23**
Pryors Rd. CM2: Gall . . . 4C **18**
Puddings Wood Dr.
CM1: Broom . . . 1E **6**
Pump Hill CM2: Gt B . . . 7F **13**
Pump La. CM1: Spr . . . 4K **7**
CM3: Dan . . . 1F **21**
Punders Fld. CM7: Brain . . . 6K **5**
Purbeck Ct. CM2: Gt B . . . 7E **12**
Purcell Cole CM1: Writ . . . 4E **10**
Purcell Rd. CM8: Wthm . . . 7G **23**
Putter Ct. CM7: Brain . . . 7H **5**
Pygot Pl. CM7: Brain . . . 3E **4**
Pyms Rd. CM2: Gall . . . 3B **18**
Pynchon M.
CM1: Spr . . . 3K **27** (2D **12**)
Pyne Ga. CM2: Gall . . . 5B **18**

Q

Quale Rd. CM2: Spr . . . 1H **13**
Quayside Ind. Est. CM9: Mal . . . 3J **25**
Quayside M. CM9: Mal . . . 5J **25**
Queenborough Gro.
CM77: Brain, Gt Not . . . 7C **4**
Queenborough La.
CM77: Brain, Gt Not . . . 7C **4**
CM77: Rayne . . . 6A **4**
Queen's Av. CM9: Mal . . . 6H **25**
Queens Ct. CM9: Mal . . . 5H **25**
Queensland Cres.
CM1: Chelm . . . 7D **6**
Queen's Rd.
CM2: Chelm . . . 5K **27** (3D **12**)
Queens Rd. CM7: Brain . . . 2F **5**
Queen St.
CM2: Chelm . . . 7F **27** (4A **12**)
CM9: Mal . . . 5H **25**
CO6: Cogg . . . 2C **26**
Quest Pl. CM9: Mal . . . 4H **25**
Quilberry Dr. CM77: Brain . . . 7D **4**
Quilp Dr. CM1: Chelm . . . 5E **6**
Quinion Cl. CM1: Chelm . . . 5C **6**
Quorn, The CM4: Inga . . . 5B **24**

R

Rachael Ct. CM2: Chelm . . . 6H **27**
Raeburn Ct. CM1: Spr . . . 6K **7**
Ragley Cl. CM77: Gt Not . . . 2A **4**
Railway Sq.
CM1: Chelm . . . 3F **27** (2A **12**)
Railway St.
CM1: Chelm . . . 3F **27** (2A **12**)
CM7: Brain . . . 4G **5**
Rainbow Mead CM3: Hat P . . . 1H **9**
Rainbow M. CM9: H'bri . . . 2G **25**
Rainsford Av. CM1: Chelm . . . 2K **11**
Rainsford La. CM1: Chelm . . . 3K **11**
Rainsford Rd.
CM1: Chelm . . . 3F **27** (2K **11**)
Ramsey Cl. CM9: H'bri . . . 3K **25**
Ramshaw Dr. CM2: Spr . . . 2F **13**
Rana Ct. CM7: Brain . . . 3F **5**
Rana Dr. CM7: Brain . . . 3F **5**
Randall Cl. CM6: Gt Dun . . . 3C **22**
CM8: Wthm . . . 7H **23**
Randolph Cl. CM9: Mal . . . 7G **25**
Randulph Ter. CM1: Spr . . . 2D **12**
Ranger Hgts. *CM7: Brain . . . 4F 5*
(off Swan Side)
Ransomes Way
CM1: Chelm . . . 1G **27** (1B **12**)
Ranulph Way CM3: Hat P . . . 2K **9**
Raphael Dr. CM1: Spr . . . 5A **8**
Ratcliff Ct. CO5: K'dn . . . 7A **26**
Ratcliffe Ga. CM1: Spr . . . 4B **8**
Ravel Av. CM8: Wthm . . . 7H **23**
Ravensbourne Dr.
CM1: Chelm . . . 4J **11**
Ray, The CM1: Spr . . . 7K **7**
Rayleigh Cl. CM7: Brain . . . 3J **5**
RAYNE . . . **5A 4**
Rayne Hall Ind. Est.
CM77: Rayne . . . 5A **4**
Rayne Rd. CM7: Brain . . . 4D **4**
CM77: Brain, Rayne . . . 5A **4**
Readers Ct. CM2: Gt B . . . 7E **12**
Rectory Chase CM2: Sando . . . 7J **13**
Rectory Cl. CM4: Inga . . . 3C **24**
Rectory La.
CM1: Chelm . . . 1G **27** (1B **12**)
CM8: Riven . . . 1J **23**
Rectory Rd. CM1: Writ . . . 5F **11**
Redbond Lodge CM6: Gt Dun . . . 4C **22**
Redcliffe Rd.
CM2: Chelm . . . 7F **27** (4A **12**)
Redgates Pl. CM2: Chelm . . . 1D **12**
Redmayne Dr. CM2: Chelm . . . 5K **11**
Redruth Cl. CM1: Spr . . . 7K **7**
Redshank Dr.
CM9: H'bri, Mal . . . 2K **25**
Redwood Cl. CM8: Wthm . . . 1J **23**
Redwood Dr. CM1: Writ . . . 4D **10**
Reed Mdws. CM7: Brain . . . 6H **5**
Regal Cl. CM2: Chelm . . . 5D **12**
Regatta Way CM9: Mal . . . 7J **25**
Regency Cl. CM2: Chelm . . . 2D **12**
Regency Ct. CM9: H'bri . . . 2H **25**
Regina Rd.
CM1: Chelm . . . 2J **27** (2C **12**)
Rembrandt Gro. CM1: Spr . . . 6K **7**
Remembrance Av.
CM3: Hat P . . . 2J **9**
Reminder Cl. CM9: Mal . . . 7J **25**
Rennie Pl. CM2: Spr . . . 2H **13**
Rennie Wlk. CM9: H'bri . . . 3K **25**
Renoir Pl. CM1: Spr . . . 5A **8**
Repertor Dr. CM9: Mal . . . 7J **25**
Retreat, The CM8: Wthm . . . 5J **23**
Rex Mott Ct. CM8: Wthm . . . 4H **23**
Reynards Ct. CM2: Gt B . . . 7F **13**
Richards Cl. CM8: Wthm . . . 5H **23**
Richardson Pl. CM1: Chelm . . . 2K **11**
Richardson Wlk. *CM8: Wthm . . . 4K 23*
(off Abercorn Way)
Richmond Rd. CM2: Spr . . . 1G **13**
Rickstones Rd.
CM8: Riven, Wthm . . . 2H **23**
Riddiford Dr. CM1: Chelm . . . 1K **11**
Ridge, The CM3: Lit B . . . 2G **15**
Ridgeway CM4: Inga . . . 6B **24**
CM9: Mal . . . 7H **25**
Ridgeway, The CM7: Brain . . . 6G **5**
Ridgewell Av. CM1: Chelm . . . 1K **11**
Ridings, The CM2: Gt B . . . 6D **12**
Ridings Av. CM77: Gt Not . . . 1A **4**
Ridley Rd. CM1: Broom . . . 4G **7**
Riffhams Chase CM3: Lit B . . . 4E **14**
Riffhams Dr. CM2: Gt B . . . 6G **13**
Riffhams La. CM3: Dan, Lit B . . . 5E **14**
Rifle Hill CM7: Brain . . . 6F **5**
Rignals La. CM2: Gall . . . 4C **18**
Rivenhall Oaks Golf Cen. . . . **1K 23**
River Cotts. CM3: Bor . . . 4G **9**
River Mead CM7: Brain . . . 3G **5**
Rivermead Ga.
CM1: Chelm . . . 1H **27** (1B **12**)
Rivermead Ind. Est.
CM1: Chelm . . . 1H **27** (1B **12**)
Riverside
CM2: Chelm . . . 3K **27** (2C **12**)
CM6: Gt Dun . . . 3D **22**
Riverside Ice & Leisure Cen.
Chelmsford . . . 3J 27 (3C 12)
Riverside Ind. Est. CM9: Mal . . . 4G **25**
Riverside Maltings
CO6: Cogg . . . 3C **26**
Riverside Pl. CM1: Writ . . . 4H **11**
Riverside Retail Pk.
CM1: Chelm . . . 2K **27** (2C **12**)
Riverside Way CO5: K'dn . . . 7B **26**
River Vw. CM7: Brain . . . 6E **4**
(not continuous)
CM8: Wthm . . . 6J **23**
Riverview CO5: K'dn . . . 6B **26**
Robert Cl. CM2: Spr . . . 1F **13**
Roberts Ct. CM2: Gt B . . . 6F **13**
Robinsbridge Rd. CO6: Cogg . . . 2B **26**
Robinson Ga. CM1: Spr . . . 3K **7**
Robin Way CM2: Chelm . . . 1B **18**
Robjohns Ho.
CM2: Chelm . . . 4K **27** (3C **12**)
Robjohns Rd. CM1: Wid . . . 5J **11**
Rochester Cl. CM7: Brain . . . 3K **5**
Rochford Rd.
CM2: Chelm . . . 6J **27** (4C **12**)
(not continuous)
Roding Ct. CM7: Brain . . . 6K **5**
Rodney Gdns. CM7: Brain . . . 3J **5**
Rodney Way CM1: Wid . . . 6J **11**
Roland Cl. CM1: Broom . . . 5G **7**
Rollestons CM1: Writ . . . 5D **10**
Rolley La. CO5: K'dn . . . 7B **26**
Roman Cl. CM9: H'bri . . . 3G **25**
Roman Ct. CM7: Brain . . . 6J **5**
Romanhurst CM9: H'bri . . . 3H **25**
Roman Rd.
CM2: Chelm . . . 7H **27** (4B **12**)
CM4: Inga . . . 6A **24**
CM4: Marg . . . 7C **16**, 1E **24**
Romans Pl. CM1: Writ . . . 4F **11**
Romans Way CM1: Writ . . . 4F **11**
Romney Cl. CM7: Bock . . . 1E **4**
Rookery Cl. CM3: Hat P . . . 1J **9**
Rookes Cres. CM1: Chelm . . . 4K **11**
Roothings, The CM9: H'bri . . . 2J **25**
Roper's Chase CM1: Writ . . . 6D **10**
Rope Wlk. CM9: Mal . . . 5H **25**
Rosebay Cl. CM8: Wthm . . . 3F **23**
Rosebery Rd.
CM2: Chelm . . . 7H **27** (5B **12**)
Rose Gdns. CM7: Brain . . . 5G **5**
Rose Glen CM2: Chelm . . . 6C **12**
Rose Hill CM7: Brain . . . 5G **5**
Roselawn Flds. CM1: Broom . . . 4G **7**
Rosemary Av. CM7: Brain . . . 3E **4**
Rosemary Cl. CM6: Gt Dun . . . 3B **22**
Rosemary Cres.
CM6: Gt Dun . . . 3B **22**
Rosemary La. CM6: Gt Dun . . . 3B **22**
Roslings Cl. CM1: Chelm . . . 6C **6**
Rossendale CM1: Chelm . . . 4J **11**
Rosseter Cl. CM2: Gt B . . . 6D **12**
Rosslyn Ter. *CO5: K'dn . . . 6B 26*
(off Station Rd.)
Rothbury Rd. CM1: Chelm . . . 4H **11**
Rothesay Av. CM2: Chelm . . . 5A **12**
Rothmans Av. CM2: Gt B . . . 7E **12**
Rothmans Pl. CM2: Gt B . . . 6E **12**
Roughtons CM2: Gall . . . 3C **18**
Rous Chase CM2: Gall . . . 5B **18**
Rowan Dr. CM9: H'bri . . . 2K **25**
Rowan Way CM3: Hat P . . . 2J **9**
CM6: Gt Dun . . . 3B **22**
CM8: Wthm . . . 1J **23**
Roxwell Av. CM1: Chelm . . . 2H **11**
Roxwell Rd.
CM1: Chelm, Writ . . . 1C **10**
Royal Ct. CM9: Mal . . . 6H **25**
Rubens Ga. CM1: Spr . . . 5A **8**
Ruby Link CM2: Gt B . . . 7D **12**
Rue de Jeunes CM7: Brain . . . 5F **5**
Rumsey Flds. CM3: Dan . . . 6H **15**
Rumsey Row CM1: Writ . . . 4F **11**
Running Mare La.
CM2: Chelm, Gall . . . 3A **18**
Runsell Cl. CM3: Dan . . . 6H **15**
RUNSELL GREEN . . . **6H 15**
Runsell La. CM3: Dan . . . 5H **15**
Runsell Vw. CM3: Dan . . . 5J **15**
Rurik Ct. CM9: Mal . . . 7G **25**
Rushleydale CM1: Spr . . . 7K **7**
Rushmoor Dr.
CM7: Brain, Tye G . . . 6H **5**
Ruskin Rd. CM2: Chelm . . . 3E **12**
Ruskins, The CM77: Rayne . . . 6A **4**
Russell Cl. CM8: Wthm . . . 7H **23**
Russell Gdns. CM2: Chelm . . . 2A **18**
Russell Way CM1: Wid . . . 6J **11**
Russet Cl. CM7: Brain . . . 6G **5**
Russets CM2: Gall . . . 3D **18**
Rustic Cl. CM7: Brain . . . 4J **5**
Rutherfords CM1: Broom . . . 3G **7**
Rutland Gdns. CM7: Brain . . . 3G **5**
Rutland Rd. CM1: Chelm . . . 6F **7**
Rydal Dr. CM9: Mal . . . 7J **25**
Rydal Way CM77: Gt Not . . . 2B **4**
Rye Cl. CM3: Hat P . . . 2J **9**
Rye Fld., The CM3: Lit B . . . 2F **15**
Rye Grass Way CM7: Brain . . . 6H **5**
Rye Mill La. CO5: Fee . . . 5C **26**
Rye Wlk. CM4: Inga . . . 5B **24**
Ryle, The CM1: Writ . . . 5E **10**
Rysley CM3: Lit B . . . 1F **15**

S

Sackville Cl. CM1: Chelm . . . 2J **11**
Saddle Ri. CM1: Spr . . . 4K **7**
Saddlers Cl. CM77: Gt Not . . . 1A **4**
Saffron Cft. CM9: Mal . . . 5F **25**
St Andrew's Rd. CM3: Hat P . . . 1J **9**
St Andrews Rd. CM3: Bor . . . 4F **9**
St Annes Cl. CO6: Cogg . . . 2D **26**
St Anne's Ct. CM2: Chelm . . . 3K **27**
St Anne's Pl.
CM2: Chelm . . . 3K **27** (2C **12**)
St Anthony's Dr. CM2: Chelm . . . 7C **12**
St Augustine's Way CM1: Spr . . . 6K **7**
St Catherine's Rd.
CM1: Chelm . . . 3J **11**
St Cleres Hall Pit CM3: Lit B . . . 5C **14**
St Cleres Way CM3: Dan . . . 6F **15**
St Edmunds Cft.
CM6: Gt Dun . . . 3D **22**
St Edmunds Flds.
CM6: Gt Dun . . . 2D **22**
St Edmunds La. CM6: Gt Dun . . . 2D **22**
St Fabian's Dr. CM1: Chelm . . . 1J **11**
St Francis Wlk. *CM7: Brain . . . 2G 5*
(off Elizabeth Lockhart Way)
St Giles Cl. CM9: Mal . . . 5F **25**

St Giles Cres. CM9: Mal . . . 5F 25
St Giles Leper Hospital (ruins) . . . 5F 25
St James Pk. CM1: Chelm . . . 1H 11
St James Rd. CM7: Brain . . . 2F 5
St John's Av. CM2: Chelm . . . 5B 12
St Johns Av. CM7: Brain . . . 5F 5
St John's Ct. CM2: Chelm . . . 6K 11
St Johns Ct.
CM2: Chelm . . . 7G 27 (4B 12)
St John's Grn. CM1: Writ . . . 4F 11
St John's Rd. CM1: Writ . . . 4F 11
CM2: Chelm . . . 7G 27 (4B 12)
St Lawrence Ct. CM7: Brain . . . 4F 5
St Luke Ct. *CM7: Brain . . . 4E 4*
(off Old St Michaels Dr.)
St Margaret's Rd.
CM2: Chelm . . . 2E 12
St Marys Cl. CM2: Gt B . . . 7F 13
St Mary's Ct. *CM9: Mal . . . 5J 25*
(off Mill Rd.)
St Mary's La. CM9: Mal . . . 5J 25
St Mary's Mead CM1: Broom . . . 4F 7
St Mary's Rd. CM7: Brain . . . 4H 5
CO5: K'dn . . . 7B 26
St Mary's Sq. CO5: K'dn . . . 7A 26
St Michael's Ct. *CM7: Brain . . . 5F 5*
(off South St.)
ST MICHAEL'S HOSPITAL . . . 4D 4
St Michael's La. CM7: Brain . . . 5F 5
St Michaels M. CM7: Brain . . . 5F 5
St Michael's Rd. CM2: Chelm . . . 5B 12
CM7: Brain . . . 5F 5
St Michael's Wlk. CM2: Gall . . . 4C 18
St Mildreds Rd. CM2: Chelm . . . 5B 12
St Nazaire Rd. CM1: Chelm . . . 6D 6
St Nicholas Cl. CM8: Wthm . . . 2H 23
St Nicholas Rd. CM8: Wthm . . . 2H 23
St Nicholas Way CO6: Cogg . . . 1C 26
St Pauls M. CM9: H'bri . . . 3K 25
St Peter's Av. CM9: Mal . . . 5G 25
St Peter's Cl. CM7: Brain . . . 4F 5
ST PETER'S HOSPITAL . . . 5G 25
St Peter's in the Flds.
CM7: Brain . . . 3F 5
St Peter's Rd. CM1: Chelm . . . 3J 11
CM7: Brain . . . 3F 5
CO6: Cogg . . . 1D 26
St Peter's Wlk. CM7: Brain . . . 4F 5
St Swithins Cotts.
CM2: Howe G . . . 3J 19
St Thomas Ct. *CM7: Brain . . . 4E 4*
(off Old St Michaels Dr.)
St Vincent Chase CM7: Brain . . . 2H 5
St Vincents Rd. CM2: Chelm . . . 5B 12
Salcombe Rd. CM7: Brain . . . 6J 5
Salcott Creek Ct. CM7: Brain . . . 6K 5
Salerno Way CM1: Chelm . . . 6D 6
Salmon Pde.
CM1: Chelm . . . 2H 27 (2B 12)
Salter Pl. CM2: Spr . . . 3F 13
Samian Cl. CM9: H'bri . . . 2G 25
Samphire Cl. CM8: Wthm . . . 3F 23
Samuel Mnr. CM2: Spr . . . 2F 13
Sanderling Gdns. CM9: H'bri . . . 2K 25
Sandford Mill La.
CM2: Gt B, Spr . . . 5H 13
Sandford Mill Rd. CM2: Spr . . . 3G 13
(Chelmer Village Way)
CM2: Spr . . . 3F 13
(Pollards Grn.)
Sandford Rd. CM2: Chelm . . . 2D 12
SANDON . . . 7J 13
Sandon Brook Pl.
CM2: Sando . . . 5A 14
Sandon Grn. CM2: Sando . . . 7J 13
Sandon Hall Bridleway
CM2: Howe G, Sando . . . 3K 19
SANDON INTERCHANGE . . . 6K 13
Sandon (Park & Ride) . . . 5K 13
Sandpiper Cl. CM9: H'bri . . . 2K 25
Sandpiper Wlk. CM2: Chelm . . . 7C 12
Sandpit La. CM7: Brain . . . 4F 5
Sandringham Pl.
CM2: Chelm . . . 4K 27 (3C 12)
Sandwich Cl. CM7: Bock . . . 1E 4
Sassoon Way CM9: Mal . . . 6H 25
Saul's Av. CM8: Wthm . . . 6J 23
Sauls Bri. Cl. CM8: Wthm . . . 6K 23
Saunders Av. CM7: Brain . . . 4E 4
Savernake Rd. CM1: Chelm . . . 4J 11
Sawkins Av. CM2: Gt B . . . 7D 12
Sawkins Cl. CM2: Gt B . . . 7D 12
Sawkins Gdns. CM2: Gt B . . . 7D 12
Sawney Brook CM1: Writ . . . 4E 10
Saxon Bank CM7: Brain . . . 5H 5
Saxon Ct. *CM9: Mal . . . 4H 25*
(off Bull La.)
Saxon Dr. CM8: Wthm . . . 3G 23
Saxon Pl. CO5: K'dn . . . 6B 26
Saxon Way CM1: Broom . . . 5G 7
CM9: Mal . . . 6J 25
Saywell Brook CM2: Spr . . . 3G 13
Scarletts Cl. CM8: Wthm . . . 7J 23
School La. CM1: Broom . . . 4E 6
School M. CO6: Cogg . . . 2B 26
School Vw. CM7: Brain . . . 5E 4
School Vw. Rd. CM1: Chelm . . . 2K 11
School Wlk. CM7: Brain . . . 4F 5
Scotfield M. CM8: Wthm . . . 5H 23
Scott Cl. CM7: Brain . . . 7G 5
Scotts Wlk. *CM1: Chelm . . . 7C 6*
(off Roslings Cl.)
Scraley Rd. CM9: H'bri . . . 1K 25
Scrubs Wood Nature Reserve
. . . 5H 15
Scylla Cl. CM9: H'bri . . . 1K 25
Seabrook Gdns. CM3: Bor . . . 3G 9
Seabrook Rd. CM2: Gt B . . . 7G 13
Searle Cl. CM2: Gt B . . . 6D 12
Second Av. CM1: Chelm . . . 7F 7
Sedgefield Way CM7: Brain . . . 6H 5
Seven Ash Grn. CM1: Spr . . . 7H 7
Seventh Av. CM1: Chelm . . . 6G 7
Seymour St. CM2: Chelm . . . 3A 12
Shakespeare Cl. CM7: Brain . . . 7G 5
Shakespeare Dr. CM9: Mal . . . 7H 25
Shakeston Cl. CM1: Writ . . . 5F 11
Shalford Lodge CM1: Chelm . . . 4G 7
Shalford Rd. CM77: Rayne . . . 4A 4
Shardelow Av. CM1: Spr . . . 5A 8
Sharpington Cl. CM2: Gall . . . 3C 18
Shaw Rd. CM8: Wthm . . . 1H 23
Shearers Way CM3: Bor . . . 3G 9
Sheene Gro. CM7: Brain . . . 2K 5
Sheepcotes CM2: Spr . . . 6C 8
Sheldrick Link CM2: Spr . . . 1H 13
Shelduck Cres. CM77: Gt Not . . . 3B 4
Shelley Cl. CM9: Mal . . . 7H 25
Shelley Rd. CM2: Chelm . . . 3D 12
Shelley Wlk. CM7: Brain . . . 7G 5
Sheppard Dr. CM2: Spr . . . 1G 13
Sherborne Rd. CM1: Spr . . . 7J 7
Sheringham Dr. CM77: Gt Not . . . 1B 4
Sherpa Path CM9: H'bri . . . 2J 25
Sherwood Dr. CM1: Chelm . . . 4H 11
Sherwood Way CO5: Fee . . . 5C 26
Shire Cl. CM1: Spr . . . 5A 8
Shire Ga.
CM2: Chelm . . . 5F 27 (3A 12)
Shires Cl. CM77: Gt Not . . . 1A 4
Shooters Way CM7: Brain . . . 5F 5
Shortridge Ct. CM8: Wthm . . . 6G 23
Shropshire Cl. CM2: Gt B . . . 1F 19
Shrubberies, The CM1: Writ . . . 5D 10
Shrublands Cl.
CM2: Chelm . . . 4K 27 (3C 12)
Sidmouth Rd. CM1: Spr . . . 6K 7
Sidney Pl. CM1: Spr . . . 5B 8
Silks Way CM7: Brain . . . 5F 5
Silver St. CM9: Mal . . . 4G 25
Silvester Way CM2: Spr . . . 1H 13
Simmonds Way CM3: Dan . . . 5H 15
Siward Rd. CM8: Wthm . . . 6F 23
Six Bells Ct. CM7: Brain . . . 2F 5
Sixth Av. CM1: Chelm . . . 6G 7
Skerry Ri. CM1: Chelm . . . 5G 7
Skiddaw Cl. CM77: Gt Not . . . 1C 4
Skinner's La. CM2: Gall . . . 3B 18
Skipper Ct. CM7: Brain . . . 7F 5
Skitts Hill CM7: Brain . . . 6G 5
Skitts Hill Ind. Est.
CM7: Brain . . . 6H 5
Skreens Ct. CM1: Chelm . . . 1H 11
Skylark Wlk. CM2: Chelm . . . 1B 18
Skyline 120 CM77: Gt Not . . . 7B 4
Slade's La. CM2: Gall . . . 3A 18
Slough Ho. Cl. CM7: Brain . . . 6K 5
Slough Rd. CM3: Dan . . . 4K 21
Smithers Dr. CM2: Gt B . . . 7G 13
Smith Hughes Cl. CM1: Chelm . . . 7E 6
Smiths Fld. CM77: Rayne . . . 5A 4
Sneezum Wlk. CM8: Wthm . . . 7G 23
Snelling Gro. CM2: Gt B . . . 7F 13
Snowberry Ct. CM7: Brain . . . 3K 5
Snowberry Rd. CM6: Gt Dun . . . 3A 22
Snowdrop Cl. CM1: Spr . . . 5K 7
CM8: Wthm . . . 2G 23
Somerset Pl. CM1: Chelm . . . 5F 7
Sorrel Gro. CM77: Gt Not . . . 1A 4
Southborough Rd.
CM2: Chelm . . . 7F 27 (5A 12)
Southcote Rd. CM8: Wthm . . . 2H 23
South Ct. CM4: Inga . . . 4D 24
Southend Rd.
CM2: Gt B, Howe G . . . 1H 19
CM9: Wdhm M . . . 1K 21
Southey Cl. CM9: H'bri . . . 3K 25
South Hill Cl. CM3: Dan . . . 7F 15
South Ho. Chase CM9: Mal . . . 7K 25
Southlands Chase
CM2: Howe G . . . 4A 20
Sth. Primrose Hill
CM1: Chelm . . . 2K 11
South St. CM7: Brain . . . 5F 5
South Vw. CM6: Gt Dun . . . 4B 22
Southview Rd. CM3: Dan . . . 7F 15
Southwood Chase CM3: Dan . . . 2J 21
Sovereign Cl. CM7: Brain . . . 3K 5
Sowerberry Cl. CM1: Chelm . . . 5E 6
Spalding Av. CM1: Chelm . . . 7D 6
Spalding Cl. CM7: Brain . . . 3E 4
Spalding Ct.
CM1: Chelm . . . 3F 27 (2A 12)
Spalding Way CM2: Gt B . . . 5F 13
Sparkey Cl. CM8: Wthm . . . 7J 23
Spa Rd. CM8: Wthm . . . 3G 23
CO5: Fee . . . 6D 26
Speckled Wood Ct. CM7: Brain . . . 7E 4
Speedwell Cl. CM8: Wthm . . . 2F 23
Spencer Cl. CM9: Mal . . . 7H 25
Spenlow Dr. CM1: Chelm . . . 5C 6
Spinks La. CM8: Wthm . . . 5G 23
Spinney, The CM3: Hat P . . . 2K 9
CM7: Brain . . . 6J 5
Spires, The CM2: Gt B . . . 7F 13
Spital Rd. CM9: Mal . . . 6F 25
Splash Ct. CM7: Brain . . . 5F 5
Spooner Cl. CM2: Gt B . . . 5D 12
Sporhams La. CM2: Sando . . . 2B 20
CM3: Dan . . . 2B 20
Spots Wlk. CM2: Gall . . . 3D 18
Spread Eagle Pl. CM4: Inga . . . 3D 24
Springbok Ho. CM2: Gt B . . . 1F 19
Spring Cl. CM3: Lit B . . . 7K 9
Spring Elms La. CM3: Lit B . . . 2G 15
SPRINGFIELD . . . 5A 8
Springfield Basin
CM2: Chelm . . . 5K 27
Springfield Cotts. CM9: H'bri . . . 2H 25
Springfield Grn. CM1: Spr . . . 1D 12
Springfield Hall La. CM1: Spr . . . 6H 7
(not continuous)
Springfield Lyons App.
CM2: Spr . . . 6B 8
Springfield Pk. Av.
CM2: Chelm . . . 3D 12
Springfield Pk. Hill
CM2: Chelm . . . 3D 12
Springfield Pk. La.
CM2: Chelm . . . 2E 12
Springfield Pk. Pde.
CM2: Chelm . . . 3D 12
Springfield Pk. Rd.
CM2: Chelm . . . 3D 12
Springfield Pl. CM1: Spr . . . 7J 7
SPRINGFIELD PRIVATE HOSPITAL
. . . 6J 7
Springfield Rd. CM1: Spr . . . 3C 12
CM2: Chelm, Spr
. . . 5J 27 (3C 12)
Springfields CM6: Gt Dun . . . 4B 22
CM77: Brain . . . 5C 4
Spring La. CM9: H'bri . . . 3J 25
Springmead CM77: Brain . . . 1C 4
Spring Pond Cl. CM2: Gt B . . . 5E 12
Spring Ri. CM2: Gall . . . 4C 18
Springwood Ct. CM7: Brain . . . 4D 4
Springwood Dr. CM7: Brain . . . 3C 4
Springwood Ind. Est.
CM7: Brain . . . 4C 4
Spruce Av. CM6: Gt Dun . . . 3A 22
Spruce Cl. CM8: Wthm . . . 2J 23
Spurgeon Pl. CO5: K'dn . . . 7B 26
Square, The CM4: Marg . . . 6E 16
CM6: Gt Dun . . . 3A 22
CM9: H'bri . . . 2H 25
CM77: Gt Not . . . 2A 4
Squirrells Ct. CM1: Chelm . . . 7E 6
Stablecroft CM1: Spr . . . 4K 7
Stacey Ct. CM6: Gt Dun . . . 3B 22
Stafford Cres. CM7: Brain . . . 3K 5
Stainer Cl. CM8: Wthm . . . 7H 23
Standrums CM6: Gt Dun . . . 4C 22
Stanes Rd. CM7: Bock . . . 1F 5
Stanley Ri. CM2: Spr . . . 2F 13
Stansted Cl. CM1: Chelm . . . 4J 11
Stanstrete Fld. CM77: Gt Not . . . 3A 4
Stapleford Cl.
CM2: Chelm . . . 6F 27 (4A 12)
Star La. CM4: Inga . . . 3D 24
CM6: Gt Dun . . . 3C 22
Station App. CM7: Brain . . . 5F 5
Station La. CM4: Inga . . . 4C 24
Station M. CM8: Wthm . . . 3J 23
Station Rd. CM3: Hat P . . . 1H 9
CM6: Gt Dun . . . 4D 22
CM7: Brain . . . 5F 5
CM8: Wthm . . . 3J 23
CM9: Mal . . . 4H 25
CO5: K'dn . . . 6B 26
Station Rd. Ind. Est.
CM6: Gt Dun . . . 4D 22
Steamer Ter.
CM1: Chelm . . . 3F 27 (2A 12)
Stebbens Way CM9: H'bri . . . 3J 25
Steen Cl. CM4: Inga . . . 3C 24
Steeple Cl. CM9: H'bri . . . 2K 25
Steerforth Cl. CM1: Chelm . . . 5C 6
Stepfield CM8: Wthm . . . 4K 23
Stephenson Rd. CM7: Brain . . . 6G 5
Stevens Rd. CM8: Wthm . . . 5G 23
Stewart Rd. CM2: Chelm . . . 7A 12
Stilemans Wood CM77: Cres . . . 6K 5
Stirrup Cl. CM1: Spr . . . 5K 7
Stock Chase CM9: H'bri . . . 2J 25
Stock Farm La. CM77: Rayne . . . 6A 4
Stock La. CM4: Inga . . . 3D 24
Stock Rd. CM2: Gall, W Han . . . 3A 18
Stock Ter. CM9: H'bri . . . 2J 25
Stonebridge Wlk.
CM2: Chelm . . . 5H 27 (3B 12)
Stone Cl. CM7: Brain . . . 5F 5
Stonegate CM4: Inga . . . 4D 24
Stoneham St. CO6: Cogg . . . 2B 26
Stone Path Dr. CM3: Hat P . . . 1H 9
Storms Way CM2: Spr . . . 3H 13
Stortford Rd. CM6: Gt Dun . . . 4A 22
Stour Ct. CM7: Brain . . . 6K 5
Stourton Rd. CM8: Wthm . . . 3G 23
Strawberry Cl. CM7: Brain . . . 6G 5
Street, The CM2: Gall . . . 4B 18
CM3: Hat P . . . 1H 9
CM77: Rayne . . . 5A 4
Street Ind. Est., The
CM9: H'bri . . . 2J 25
Strudwick Cl. CM7: Brain . . . 5F 5
Strutt Cl. CM3: Hat P . . . 1J 9
Stuart Cl. CM2: Gt B . . . 6H 13
Stuarts Way CM7: Brain . . . 5H 5
Stubbs La. CM7: Brain . . . 5J 5
Stump La. CM1: Spr . . . 1D 12
Suffolk Dr. CM2: Spr . . . 1G 13
Suffolk Rd. CM9: Mal . . . 6F 25
Summerfields CM4: Inga . . . 4D 24
Summerleaze Ct. CM77: Brain . . . 1C 4
Sunbank CM6: Gt Dun . . . 4D 22
Sunbury Way CM9: Mal . . . 7G 25
Sunflower Cl. CM1: Spr . . . 6A 8
Sun Lido Sq. Gdns.
CM77: Brain . . . 5C 4
Sunningdale Fall CM3: Hat P . . . 1K 9
Sunningdale Rd. CM1: Chelm . . . 1J 11
Sunnyside CM7: Brain . . . 4E 4
Sunnyway CM3: Dan . . . 3G 21
Sunrise Av. CM1: Chelm . . . 7F 7
Sussex Cl. CM3: Bor . . . 4G 9
Sutherland Ho.
CM1: Chelm . . . 1F 27 (1A 12)
Sutor Cl. CM8: Wthm . . . 5G 23
Sutton Mead CM2: Spr . . . 1G 13
Swallow Path CM2: Chelm . . . 2B 18
Swanbridge Ind. Pk.
CM8: Wthm . . . 3J 23
Swan Cl. CM3: Hat P . . . 1H 9
Swan Ct. CM9: H'bri . . . 3J 25
Swan La. CM4: Marg, Stock . . . 7G 17
Swan Side CM7: Brain . . . 4F 5
Swans Pasture CM1: Spr . . . 6J 7
Swan St. CO5: K'dn . . . 6C 26
Swan Vale Ind. Est.
CM8: Wthm . . . 3K 23
Swan Yd. CO6: Cogg . . . 2C 26
Swift Cl. CM7: Brain . . . 7G 5
Swifts Path CM9: H'bri . . . 1K 25
Swinbornes Cft. CO6: Cogg . . . 3A 26

Swinbourne Dr. CM7: Brain 4D **4**
Swiss Av.
CM1: Chelm 1F **27** (1K **11**)
Sycamore Cl. CM8: Wthm 1J **23**
Sycamore Gro. CM7: Brain 5D **4**
Sycamore Rd. CM9: H'bri 1J **25**
Sycamore Way CM2: Chelm 7C **12**
Sydner Cl. CM2: Gt B 1G **19**
Sylvan Cl. CM2: Chelm 7B **12**
Symmons Cl. CM77: Rayne 6A **4**

T

Taber Pl. CM8: Wthm 3K **23**
Tabor Av. CM7: Brain 4E **4**
Tabors Av. CM2: Gt B 5F **13**
Tabor's Hill CM2: Gt B 6F **13**
Tailors Cl. CM77: Gt Not 1B **4**
Tait M. CM9: Mal 5H **25**
Tamar Av. CM8: Wthm 4G **23**
Tamar Ri. CM1: Spr 6H **7**
Tamdown Way CM7: Brain 3C **4**
Tanfield Tye CM2: W Han 7E **18**
Tanners Mdw. CM7: Brain 5K **5**
Tapestry Wlk. CM7: Brain 5K **5**
Tapley Rd. CM1: Chelm 5E **6**
Tasman Ct. CM1: Chelm 7D **6**
Tattersall Way CM1: Wid 6J **11**
Taunton Rd. CM1: Spr 7K **7**
Taverners Wlk.
CM8: Wthm 2H **23**
Tavistock Rd. CM1: Spr 7K **7**
Taylor Av. CM1: Chelm 7D **6**
Taylor Way CM2: Gt B 7F **13**
Teak Wlk. CM8: Wthm 2J **23**
Teal Cl. CM77: Gt Not 3A **4**
Teal Way CO5: K'dn 7C **26**
Tees Cl. CM8: Wthm 4G **23**
Tees Rd. CM1: Spr 6H **7**
Teign Dr. CM8: Wthm 4F **23**
Telford Pl. CM1: Spr 1D **12**
Telford Rd. CM7: Brain 6G **5**
Templar Rd. CM7: Brain 5K **5**
Templars Cl. CM8: Wthm 2H **23**
Temple Farm Trad. Est.
CM2: W Han 7B **18**
Temple Gro. Cvn. Pk.
CM2: W Han 7C **18**
Templemead CM8: Wthm 3H **23**
Templeton Pk.
CM2: W Han 7B **18**
Temple Way CM9: H'bri 2G **25**
Ten Acre App. CM9: H'bri 2G **25**
Tennyson Cl. CM7: Brain 7F **5**
Tennyson Rd. CM1: Chelm 7E **6**
CM9: Mal 7H **25**
Tenpin
Chelmsford **6J 11**
Tenter Cl. CM7: Brain 2F **5**
Tenterfield Rd. CM9: Mal 5H **25**
Tenterfields CM6: Gt Dun 4D **22**
Terling Rd. CM8: Wthm 3F **23**
Tern Cl. CO5: K'dn 6C **26**
Terrace, The CM3: Hat P 1K **9**
Tey Rd. CO6: Cogg 1D **26**
Thackeray Cl. CM7: Brain 7G **5**
Thalatta Cl. CM9: Mal 7J **25**
Thames Av. CM1: Chelm 7B **6**
Thames Cl. CM7: Brain 6K **5**
Thatchers Way CM77: Gt Not 7C **4**
The . . . .
Names prefixed with 'The' for example 'The Avenue' are indexed under the main name such as 'Avenue, The'
Thetford Ct. CM1: Chelm 4J **11**
Third Av. CM1: Chelm 7F **7**
Thirlmere Cl. CM77: Gt Not 1C **4**
Thirslet Dr. CM9: H'bri 3K **25**
THISTLEY GREEN 1H **5**
Thistley Grn. Rd. CM7: Bock 1H **5**
(not continuous)
Thomas Cl. CM2: Spr 2F **13**
Thomas Plume's Library **4H 25**
Thorington Cl. CM77: Gt Not 2B **4**
Thorne Rd. CO5: K'dn 7A **26**
Thorpe M. CM7: Brain 4J **5**
Threadneedle St.
CM1: Chelm 4G **27** (3B **12**)
Three Mile Hill CM2: Wid 4F **17**
CM4: Chelm, Marg, Writ . . .4F **17**
Threshelfords Bus. Pk.
CO5: Fee 5D **26**
Thresher Ri. CM77: Brain 7C **4**
Thrift Wood CM3: B'acre 5G **21**
Thrift Wood Nature Reserve . . .**6J 21**
Thyme M. CM8: Wthm 3G **23**
Tiberius Gdns.
CM8: Wthm 6G **23**
Tideswell Cl. CM7: Brain 3K **5**
Tideway CM9: Mal 7J **25**
TILKEY 1B **26**
Tilkey Rd. CO6: Cogg 1B **26**
Timbers Cl. CM77: Gt Not 1A **4**
Timber Yd. *CM7: Brain 5G 5*
(off Station App.)
Timsons La. CM2: Spr 1E **12**
Tindal Sq.
CM1: Chelm 4H **27** (3B **12**)
Tindal St.
CM1: Chelm 4H **27** (3B **12**)
Tintagel Way CM9: Mal 7F **25**
Tithe Cl. CM8: Wthm 3G **23**
Tobruk Rd. CM1: Chelm 6E **6**
Tofts Chase CM3: Lit B 1F **15**
Tofts Wlk. *CM7: Brain 4F 5*
(off Swan Side)
Tor Bryan CM4: Inga 5B **24**
Torquay Rd. CM1: Spr 7J **7**
Torrington Cl. CM1: Spr 7K **7**
Tortoiseshell Way
CM7: Brain 6E **4**
Torver Cl. CM77: Gt Not 2B **4**
Totnes Wlk. CM1: Spr 6K **7**
Toulmin Rd. CM3: Hat P 1J **9**
Tourist Info. Cen.
Braintree Freeport **6J 5**
Great Dunmow **4C 22**
Maldon District **4H 25**
Witham **5J 23**
Tower Av. CM1: Chelm 1K **11**
Tower Rd. CM1: Writ 4D **10**
Towers Rd. CM9: H'bri 2K **25**
Town Cft. CM1: Chelm 7F **7**
Town End Fld. CM8: Wthm 6G **23**
Townfield St.
CM1: Chelm 3F **27** (2B **12**)
Townsend CM2: Spr 7C **8**
Traddles Ct. CM1: Chelm 6E **6**
Trafalgar Ct. CM7: Brain 3H **5**
Trafalgar Way CM7: Brain 3H **5**
Trenchard Cres. CM1: Spr 5J **7**
Trenchard Lodge CM1: Spr 5J **7**
Trent Rd. CM1: Chelm 7B **6**
CM8: Wthm 4G **23**
Trews Gdns. CO5: K'dn 6B **26**
Triangle Pl. CM9: H'bri 2J **25**
Trimble Cl. CM4: Inga 3C **24**
Trinity Cl.
CM2: Chelm 3K **27** (2D **12**)
Trinity Rd.
CM2: Chelm 3K **27** (3D **12**)
Trinovantian Way
CM7: Brain 5G **5**
Trotters Fld. CM7: Brain 4H **5**
Trotwood Cl. CM1: Chelm 5D **6**
Trueloves Grange CM4: Inga . . .4A **24**
TRUELOVES INTERCHANGE . . .**5A 24**
Trueloves La. CM4: Inga 5A **24**
Tucker Dr. CM8: Wthm 5H **23**
Tudor Av. CM1: Chelm 2A **12**
Tudor Cl. CM4: Inga 5B **24**
CM8: Wthm 6H **23**
Tufted Cl. CM77: Gt Not 3B **4**
Tugby Pl. CM1: Chelm 6D **6**
Tulip Cl. CM1: Spr 5K **7**
Tupman Cl. CM1: Chelm 6C **6**
Turkey Oaks
CM1: Spr 3K **27** (2C **12**)
Turnpike Pl. CM7: Brain 4G **5**
Turstan Rd. CM8: Wthm 6G **23**
Tusser Ct. CM2: Gt B 5D **12**
Twelve Acres CM7: Brain 4K **5**
Twin Oaks CM2: Spr 1G **13**
Twitten La. CM2: Gall 4B **18**
Twitty Fee CM3: Dan 4J **15**
Tydemans CM2: Gt B 7D **12**
(not continuous)
Tye, The CM3: E Han 7E **20**
CM4: Marg 7G **17**
Tylers Cl. CM2: Chelm 7B **12**
Tyndales La. CM3: Dan 1K **21**
Tyne Way CM1: Chelm 7C **6**
Tyrell Lodge CM2: Chelm 4K **27**
Tyrells Cl. CM2: Chelm 1E **12**
Tyrells Way CM2: Gt B 6F **13**
Tyssen Mead CM3: Bor 4F **9**
Tythe Cl. CM1: Spr 4K **7**
Tythings, The CM2: Howe G 4K **19**

U

Ullswater Cl. CM77: Gt Not 2B **4**
Ulting Rd. CM3: Hat P 2K **9**
Uplands Dr. CM1: Spr 5J **7**
Upper Acres CM8: Wthm 1H **23**
Upper Bri. Rd. CM2: Chelm 5A **12**
Upper Chase CM2: Chelm 5A **12**
Up. Mill Fld. CM6: Gt Dun 5D **22**
Up. Roman Rd.
CM2: Chelm 7H **27** (4B **12**)
Urban Hive CM77: Gt Not 7B **4**
Usborne M. CM1: Writ 4G **11**

V

Vale End CM2: Gall 3C **18**
Valentine Ct. CM7: Brain 3E **4**
Valletta Cl. CM1: Chelm 2A **12**
Valley Bri. CM1: Chelm 6G **7**
Valley Rd. CM7: Brain 3G **5**
Van Dieman's La.
CM2: Chelm 5C **12**
Van Dieman's Rd.
CM2: Chelm 7K **27** (5C **12**)
Vane Ct. CM8: Wthm 1J **23**
Vane La. CO6: Cogg 2C **26**
Vanguard Way CM7: Brain 3H **5**
Varden Cl. CM1: Chelm 6E **6**
Vauxhall Dr. CM7: Brain 5D **4**
Vellacotts CM1: Broom 5G **7**
Venmore Dr. CM6: Gt Dun 4C **22**
Venta Way CM9: Mal 7J **25**
Vermeer Ride CM1: Spr 5A **8**
Vernon Way CM7: Brain 2J **5**
Vesta Cl. CO6: Cogg 2B **26**
Viaduct Rd.
CM1: Chelm 4F **27** (3A **12**)
Viborg Gdns. CM9: Mal 7F **25**
Vicarage Cres. CM3: Hat P 1K **9**
Vicarage La. CM2: Gt B 3F **19**
Vicarage M. CM2: Gt B 7F **13**
Vicarage Rd. CM1: Rox 1A **10**
CM2: Chelm 7G **27** (6A **12**)
Victoria Ct.
CM1: Chelm 3H **27** (2B **12**)
CM7: Brain 5G 5
(off Railway St.)
CM9: Mal 5J **25**
Victoria Cres.
CM1: Chelm 2F **27** (2B **12**)
Victoria Rd.
CM1: Chelm 3G **27** (2B **12**)
CM1: Writ 4C **10**
CM2: Chelm 3G **27** (2B **12**)
CM9: Mal 4H **25**
Victoria Rd. Sth.
CM1: Chelm 4G **27** (3B **12**)
Victoria St. CM7: Brain 5F **5**
Victory Gdns. CM7: Brain 3H **5**
Viking Rd. CM9: Mal 7F **25**
Village Ga. CM2: Spr 2G **13**
Village Sq. CM2: Spr 2G **13**
Villiers Pl. CM3: Bor 4F **9**
Vineyards, The CM2: Gt B 6F **13**
CM3: Hat P 1J **9**
Violet Cl. CM1: Spr 5K **7**
Virgil Rd. CM8: Wthm 1H **23**
Virgin Active
Chelmsford . . . . .**5F 27 (3A 12)**
Virley Cl. CM9: H'bri 3K **25**
Volwycke Av. CM9: Mal 7G **25**

W

Wadham Cl. CM4: Inga 3C **24**
Wagtail Dr. CM9: H'bri 2K **25**
Wagtail Pl. CO5: K'dn 7B **26**
Wainwright Av. CM77: Brain 7D **4**
Wakelin Chase CM4: Inga 4B **24**
Wakelin Path CM9: H'bri 2K **25**
Wakelin Way CM8: Wthm 4K **23**
Waldgrooms CM6: Gt Dun 3B **22**
Walford Cl. CO6: Cogg 1C **26**
Walford Pl. CM2: Spr 3F **13**
Walford Way CO6: Cogg 2C **26**
Walkers Cl. CM1: Spr 5J **7**
Walkfares CM3: Bor 4G **9**
Wallace Binder Cl. CM9: Mal . . .6G **25**
Wallace Cres. CM2: Chelm 5C **12**
Wallaces La. CM3: Bor 1G **9**
Wallasea Gdns. CM1: Spr 7A **8**
Wall Ct. CM7: Brain 6F **5**
Wallflower Ct. CM1: Spr 6A **8**
Walnut Dr. CM8: Wthm 2J **23**
Walnut Gro. CM7: Brain 5E **4**
Walnut Wlk. CM6: Gt Dun 3A **22**
Walters Cl. CM2: Gall 3C **18**
Waltham Glen CM2: Chelm 6C **12**
Waltham Rd. CM3: Bor 1G **9**
Walton Hgts.
CM1: Chelm 2H **27** (2B **12**)
Wantz Chase CM9: Mal 5H **25**
Wantz Haven CM9: Mal 5H **25**
Wantz Rd. CM4: Marg 5D **16**
CM9: Mal 5H **25**
Warder Cl. CM6: Gt Dun 3D **22**
Wardle Way CM1: Chelm 5D **6**
Ward Path CM2: Spr 1H **13**
Warley Cl. CM7: Brain 3J **5**
Warne Av. CM7: Brain 1F **5**
Warner Cl. CM77: Rayne 6A **4**
Warner Dr. CM7: Brain 3C **4**
Warners CM6: Gt Dun 4C **22**
Warner Textile Archive (Mus.)
. . . .**5F 5**
Warren Cl. CM1: Broom 1G **7**
Warren Golf Course
Essex **4K 15**
Warren Rd. CM7: Brain 5J **5**
Warrenside CM7: Brain 7G **5**
Warwick Cl. CM7: Brain 3G **5**
CM9: Mal 6H **25**
Warwick Cres. CM9: Mal 6H **25**
Warwick Dr. CM9: Mal 6H **25**
Warwick Sq. CM1: Chelm 1K **11**
Washall Dr. CM77: Brain 7D **4**
Washington Cl. CM9: Mal 6F **25**
Washington Rd. CM9: Mal 6F **25**
Watchouse Rd. CM2: Gall 4B **18**
Waterhall Meadows Nature Reserve
. . . .**2C 14**
Waterhouse Bus. Pk.
CM1: Chelm 4K **11**
Waterhouse La. CM1: Chelm . . .4J **11**
Waterhouse St. CM1: Chelm . . .5K **11**
Waterings, The CM7: Brain 5F **5**
Waterloo La.
CM1: Chelm 4H **27** (3B **12**)
Watermill Rd. CO5: Fee 5D **26**
Waterside Bus. Pk.
CM8: Wthm 2K **23**
Waterson Va.
CM2: Chelm, Gt B 5C **12**
Wavell Cl. CM1: Spr 4J **7**
Waveney Dr. CM1: Spr 6H **7**
Waverley Bri. Ct. CM9: H'bri . . .3J **25**
Wayside CM3: Lit B 5G **15**
Wear Dr. CM1: Spr 6J **7**
(not continuous)
Weavers Cl. CM6: Gt Dun 4C **22**
CM7: Brain 4F **5**
Webb Cl. CM2: Spr 2H **13**
WEBBS FARM INTERCHANGE
. . . .**5F 17**
Weight Rd.
CM2: Chelm 4K **27** (3C **12**)
Welland Av. CM1: Chelm 7B **6**
Weller Gro. CM1: Chelm 5D **6**
Wellfield CM1: Writ 4E **10**
Wellington Cl. CM1: Chelm 7C **6**
CM7: Brain 3J **5**
Wellington Rd. CM9: Mal 5G **25**
Well La. CM2: Gall 4B **18**
CM3: Dan 7E **14**
Wellmeads CM2: Chelm 5B **12**
Wells Ct. CM1: Spr 7J **7**
CM6: Gt Dun 3B **22**
Wells Cross CM1: Chelm 3F **27**
Wells St.
CM1: Chelm 3F **27** (2A **12**)
Well Ter. CM9: H'bri 2J **25**
Wenlock Way CM9: Mal 4H **25**
Wentworth Cl. CM3: Hat P 1K **9**
Wentworth Cres. CM7: Brain 2F **5**
Wentworth Mdws. CM9: Mal . . .5G **25**
West Av. CM1: Chelm 7E **6**
West Belvedere CM3: Dan 6H **15**
Westbourne Gro. CM2: Gt B 6D **12**
W. Bowers Rd.
CM9: Wdhm W 1K **15**
West Chase CM9: Mal 4G **25**

West Ct. CM4: Inga 4C **24**
Westerdale CM1: Spr 5J **7**
Westergreen Mdw.
CM7: Brain 6E **4**
Westerings CM3: Dan 4H **21**
Westerings, The CM2: Gt B 1F **19**
Westfield Av.
CM1: Chelm 1F **27** (1A **12**)
Westfield Dr. CO6: Cogg 1C **26**
W. Hanningfield Rd.
CM2: Gt B, W Han 7E **18**
West Lawn CM2: Gall 4C **18**
Westminster Gdns.
CM7: Brain 3G **5**
West Sq. CM9: Mal 4G **25**
W. Station Ind. Est.
CM9: Mal 6F **25**
W. Station Yd. CM9: Mal 6F **25**
West St. CO6: Cogg 3A **26**
Westway CM1: Wid 5J **11**
Weymouth Rd. CM1: Spr 6K **7**
Whadden Chase CM4: Inga 4B **24**
Wharfe Cl. CM8: Wthm 4G **23**
Wharf Rd.
CM2: Chelm 5K **27** (3C **12**)
Wharton Dr. CM1: Spr 5B **8**
Wheatear Ind. Est.
CM8: Wthm 5K **23**
Wheatfield Way CM1: Chelm . . .2K **11**
Wheatley Av. CM7: Brain 4J **5**
Wheaton Rd. CM8: Wthm 4K **23**
Wheatsheaf Rd. CM7: Brain 4E **4**
Wheelwrights Yd.
CM6: Gt Dun 4C **22**
Whitebeam Cl. CM2: Wid 6K **11**
White Elm Rd.
CM3: B'acre, Dan 4H **21**
Whitegates Cl. CM77: Gt Not 2B **4**
Whitehall Ct. CM8: Wthm 4J **23**
White Hart La. CM1: Spr 4K **7**
CM2: Spr 4K **7**
White Hart Way CM6: Gt Dun . . .4C **22**
Whitehead Cl. CM1: Writ 5F **11**
White Horse La. CM8: Wthm . . .3H **23**
CM9: Mal 5G **25**
Whitehouse Cres. CM2: Gt B . . .5D **12**
White Mead CM1: Broom 2G **7**
White Post Fld. CM6: Gt Dun . . .4D **22**
Whitesbridge La.
CM4: Chelm, Marg 4H **17**
White St. CM6: Gt Dun 4C **22**
Whitethorn Gdns.
CM2: Chelm 6C **12**
Whiteways Ct. CM8: Wthm 3G **23**
Whitfield Link CM2: Chelm 6D **12**
Whitley Link CM2: Chelm 7K **11**
Whitmore Cres. CM2: Spr 2H **13**
Whyverne Cl. CM1: Spr 6K **7**
Wickfield Ash CM1: Chelm 6C **6**
Wickham Cres. CM1: Chelm 6E **6**
CM7: Brain 5G **5**
Wickham Rd. CM8: Wthm 6H **23**
Wickham's Chase CM3: Dan 4K **21**
Wickhay Cotts. CM3: Lit B 1F **15**
Wicklow Av. CM1: Chelm 6C **6**
Wicks Cl. CM7: Brain 4C **4**
Wicks Pl. CM1: Chelm 2A **12**
WIDFORD **6K 11**
Widford Chase CM2: Wid 6K **11**
Widford Cl. CM2: Wid 6K **11**
Widford Gro. CM2: Wid 6K **11**
Widford Hall La. *CM1: Wid 6J **11***
(off Tattersall Way)
Widford Ind. Est. CM1: Wid 6J **11**
(not continuous)
Widford Pk. Pl. CM2: Wid 6K **11**
Widford Rd. CM2: Wid 6K **11**
Widgeon Pl. CO5: K'dn 7B **26**
Wigeon Cl. CM77: Gt Not 3B **4**
Wiggins Vw. CM2: Spr 1H **13**
Wild Boar Fld. CM7: Brain 4K **5**
Wilkinson Pl. CM3: Hat P 2J **9**
Wilkinsons Mead CM2: Spr 1G **13**
William Porter Cl. CM1: Spr 4A **8**
Williams Dr. CM7: Brain 3F **5**
Williams Rd. CM1: Broom 3G **7**
Willingale Rd. CM7: Brain 3K **5**
Willoughby Dr. CM2: Spr 3F **13**
Willow Bank CM2: Gall 3B **18**
Willow Cl. CM1: Broom 3G **7**
Willow Cres. CM3: Hat P 2J **9**
Willow Grn. CM4: Inga 3C **24**
Willow Ri. CM8: Wthm 1J **23**
Willow Rd. CM6: Gt Dun 3B **22**
Willows, The CM1: Chelm 3A **12**
CM3: Bor 4F **9**
Willow Wlk. CM9: H'bri 2K **25**
Wilshire Av. CM2: Spr 2F **13**
Wilsons Ct. CM9: Mal 5J **25**
Wimsey Ct. CM8: Wthm 1J **23**
Winchelsea Dr. CM2: Gt B 6D **12**
Windermere Dr. CM77: Gt Not . . .1B **4**
Windley Tye CM1: Chelm 2J **11**
Windmill Cl. CM6: Gt Dun 3D **22**
Windmill Flds. CO6: Cogg 1B **26**
Windmills, The
CM1: Broom 1F **7**
Windrush Dr. CM1: Spr 6H **7**
Windsor Cl. CM8: Wthm 6H **23**
Windsor Gdns. CM7: Brain 3H **5**
Windsor Way CM1: Chelm 4J **11**
Wingate Cl. CM7: Brain 3E **4**
Wingrove Ct. CM1: Chelm 6F **7**
Winsford Way CM2: Spr 5C **8**
Winston Cl. CM7: Bock 1E **4**
Wisdoms Grn. CO6: Cogg 1D **26**
WITHAM **5J 23**
Witham Leisure Cen. **5H 23**
Witham Lodge CM8: Wthm 6F **23**
WITHAM SOUTH INTERCHANGE
. . . .**7F 23**
Witham Station (Rail) **3J 23**
Woburn Ct. CM2: Chelm 6F **27**
Wolseley Rd.
CM2: Chelm 6F **27** (4A **12**)
Wood Dale CM2: Gt B 7E **12**
Woodfield CM8: Wthm 6H **23**
Woodfield Cotts. CM9: H'bri 1K **25**
(not continuous)
Woodfield Rd. CM7: Brain 4G **5**
Woodfield Way CM3: Hat P 1J **9**
Woodhall Hill CM1: Chig S 2B **6**
Woodhall Pde. CM1: Chelm 5F **7**
Woodhall Rd. CM1: Chelm 5F **7**
Woodham Dr. CM3: Hat P 1K **9**
Woodham Walter Common
Nature Reserve **3J 15**
WOODHILL **1D 20**
Woodhill Comn. Rd.
CM3: Dan 1D **20**
Woodhill Rd.
CM2: Gt B, Sando 7H **13**
CM3: Dan 7A **14**
Woodhouse La.
CM1: Broom, Lit W 1F **7**
CM3: Lit W 1F **7**
Woodland Cl. CM3: Hat P 1J **9**
CM4: Inga 3D **24**
Woodland Rd. CM1: Chelm 1A **12**
Woodlands CM7: Brain 4H **5**
WOODLANDS PARK **2A 22**
Woodlands Pk. Dr.
CM6: Gt Dun 3A **22**
Woodlands Wlk.
CM6: Gt Dun 3A **22**
Woodlands Way CM1: Broom 1E **6**
Woodland Way CM1: E Com 1A **16**
Wood La. CM9: H'bri 2H **25**
Wood Leys CM1: Chelm 5F **7**
Wood Rd. CM9: H'bri 1J **25**
Woodroffe Cl. CM2: Spr 2G **13**
Woodrush Cl. CM7: Brain 6H **5**
Woodside CM3: Lit B 4G **15**
Woodside Cotts.
CM1: E Com 1A **16**
Woodside Way
CM6: Gt Dun, L Eas 3A **22**
Woodstock Pl. CM2: Gt B 1F **19**
Wood St. CM2: Chelm, Wid 6K **11**
Woodview Rd. CM6: Gt Dun 4B **22**
Wood Way CM77: Gt Not 1A **4**
Woolpack La. CM7: Brain 2F **5**
Worcester Cl. CM7: Brain 6G **5**
Worcester Ct. CM2: Gt B 1G **19**
Wordsworth Av. CM9: Mal 7H **25**
Wordsworth Ct. CM1: Chelm 7F **7**
Wordsworth Rd. CM7: Bock 1F **5**
Worlds End La. CO5: Fee 6C **26**
Wright Mead CM2: Spr 1H **13**
WRITTLE **4F 11**
Writtle Pk. CM1: E Com 2A **16**
Writtle Rd. CM1: Chelm 4J **11**
CM2: Chelm 4J **11**
CM4: Marg 5D **16**
Wulvesford CM8: Wthm 6F **23**
Wycke Hill CM9: Mal 6F **25**
Wycke Hill Bus. Pk.
CM9: Mal 7F **25**
Wykeham Rd. CM1: Writ 3F **11**

Y

Yard, The CM7: Brain 5G **5**
Yare Av. CM8: Wthm 3F **23**
Yarwood Rd. CM2: Chelm 3E **12**
Yeldham Lock CM2: Spr 3G **13**
Yeoman Lodge CM2: Spr 2F **13**
Yew Cl. CM8: Wthm 1K **23**
Yew Tree Cl. CM3: Hat P 1J **9**
Yewtree Gdns. CM2: Chelm 7C **12**
Yonge Cl. CM3: Bor 3F **9**
York Gdns. CM7: Brain 3H **5**
York Rd. CM2: Chelm . . .7F **27** (5A **12**)

The representation on the maps of a road, track or footpath is no evidence of the existence of a right of way.

SAFETY CAMERA INFORMATION

PocketGPSWorld.com's CamerAlert is a self-contained speed and red light camera warning system for SatNavs and Android or Apple iOS smartphones/tablets. Visit www.cameralert.com to download.

Safety camera locations are publicised by the Safer Roads Partnership which operates them in order to encourage drivers to comply with speed limits at these sites. It is the driver's absolute responsibility to be aware of and to adhere to speed limits at all times.

By showing this safety camera information it is the intention of Geographers' A-Z Map Company Ltd. to encourage safe driving and greater awareness of speed limits and vehicle speed. Data accurate at time of printing.